INTEGRATIVE
PARENTING

INTEGRATIVE PARENTING

Strategies for Raising Children Affected by Attachment Trauma

Debra Wesselmann
Cathy Schweitzer
Stefanie Armstrong

Foreword by Douglas Vincent

W. W. Norton & Company
New York • London

The discussion of the domino effect on pages 60–67 is adapted
    with permission from Ann E. Potter.
The discussion of the parenting strategy "10-20-10" on pages 39–40 is provided
    courtesy of Bryan Post, The Post Institute, http://www.postinstitute.com

Manufacturing by RR Donnelley Kendallville
Production manager: Leeann Graham

Library of Congress Cataloging-in-Publication Data

Wesselmann, Debra.
 Integrative parenting : strategies for raising children
affected by attachment trauma / Debra Wesselmann,
Catherine Schweitzer, Stefanie Armstrong; foreword
by Douglas Vincent. — First edition.
    pages cm
"A Norton professional book."
 Includes bibliographical references and index.
 ISBN 978-0-393-70817-2 (pbk.)
1. Attachment disorder in children. 2. Psychic trauma in children.
3. Eye movement desensitization and reprocessing. 4. Parenting—
Psychological aspects. I. Schweitzer, Catherine. II. Armstrong,
Stefanie. III. Title.
 RJ507.A77W46 2014
 618.92'8588—dc23

                                        2013014088

ISBN: 978-0-393-70817-2 (pbk.)

W. W. Norton & Company, Inc., 500 Fifth Avenue, New York, N.Y. 10110
www.wwnorton.com

W. W. Norton & Company Ltd., 15 Carlisle Street, London W1D 3BS

    2   3   4   5   6   7   8   9   0

To the many dedicated parents who
go "above and beyond" each day
to make a difference in the lives of their children.

Contents

Acknowledgments

WE ARE INDEBTED to the many parents who, through trial and error, have helped us in identifying the best methods of healing their hurt children. We are very grateful to our editor Deborah Malmud for her invaluable insights and suggestions. She helped us turn our manuscript into an organized and reader-friendly guide.

We wish to express our gratitude to Francine Shapiro, PhD, for developing a theoretical model and treatment that has increased compassion and deepened understanding for traumatized individuals worldwide. Thank you to Joan Lovett, MD, for many inspirational conversations and therapeutic ideas throughout the years—and for the healing provided through her storytelling method. Thanks also to Meghan Davidson, PhD, for her guidance in data collection and research over the past several years.

Thanks to Mandy Busch and Daniel Bruckner for helping found the Attachment and Trauma Center of Nebraska. Thank you to our colleague Ann Potter, PhD, for her ideas regarding the domino effect and child meltdowns. Thank you to the rest of our current team: Kris Walpus, Bonnie Sarton-Mireau, Teresa Lenzen, Ellie Fields, Maraleigh Lewandowski, and Hope Peabody for their support, wisdom, and professionalism.

Foreword

Douglas Vincent

As a parent, I have found myself on more than one chaotic moment silently reciting the 12-step Serenity Prayer: "God grant me the serenity to accept the things I cannot change; the courage to change the things I can; and the wisdom to know the difference" (originated by Reinhold Niebuhr in 1943). Raising kids in the best of circumstances is a staggering proposition. Raising traumatized children takes the challenge to another level. Serenity seems out of reach. Acceptance is impossible. Wisdom is lost in the fog. Some days I have found myself clinging to my very last thread of courage. That courage came, as it always did, from love. But for all its power, all of its intensity, it is a hard lesson to learn. Sometimes love is not enough.

It is easy to talk or write about "parenting" as if it were some isolated task that consists of throwing that switch, turning this dial, or completing a dance step that is diagrammed on the floor with a set of shoe prints each clearly labeled "right" and "left." We parents know better. Raising children is a complicated dance. The tune playing in my ear is frequently different than the music my child hears. Synchronizing the steps—matching the rhythm in my child's head—is possible if I first truly listen to the notes of my own life. That is the revelation that I found in this book, though these insights were first given to me in a series of classes provided by the authors before their curriculum found its way into print.

Recognizing that all of my life experiences, from my own childhood on, are part of who I am, how I act, and what I feel, and accepting my own imperfections for what they are, frees me to truly understand my part in this waltz as a parent. I was the victim of abuse as a child. Perhaps there is severe trauma in your past as well. Or maybe your parents, like all parents, were human and made mistakes. Whatever our histories are, we bring our own individual strengths and adaptations to all of our relationships, including our loving attempts to be the best parents we can be. This guide offers insights not only into what's going on with our children but, more importantly, what's going on inside *us*.

Understanding how a troubled child's brain works helps us likewise understand how our own minds are wired to respond. Understanding why I react and sometimes overreact to my child's behaviors gives me a chance to break the cycle of chaos. Understanding leads to acceptance, and less chaos results in a chance to feel a bit of serenity.

My triggers and my traumas are mine to understand and accept. Knowing how they influence my behaviors as a parent frees me from living through one reflexive response after another. This is the great insight I gained from the lessons in this book. I raised three children as a parent, and now I am raising a granddaughter full-time. There are unique challenges to guiding a wounded child through the maze of trauma and attachment problems. Whatever your situation, you will find yourself in these pages, and that is the key.

At one of the class sessions that I attended, one of the other overwhelmed grown-ups suddenly spoke up in the middle of the presentation, "Hey! This class is all about me!" That was a lightbulb snapping on over all of our heads—the illumination of acceptance. And that bit of light—that taste of serenity gained through knowledge—made it easier to find that wisdom we were looking for as parents, foster parents, and guardians.

This book is all about us.

Introduction

THIS BOOK IS WRITTEN for birth parents, foster parents, adoptive parents, aunts and uncles, grandpas and grandmas, and anyone else who may be raising a child who has experienced attachment loss and trauma. In addition, it serves as a resource for therapists, social workers, foster care specialists, health and human services workers, and others who are working with affected families. This guide is the collective work of therapists who treat severely traumatized and attachment-disordered children and their parents. Through data collection, research, and our work with affected families over the past several years, we have developed a model of treatment that includes a family therapist and an EMDR therapist functioning as a team, along with parenting strategies designed to help calm behaviors and improve attachment security in children.

The severe behaviors of these children frequently leave parents frightened, hurt, and overwhelmed. Parents both love and fear their adopted, foster, and biological children and want to know how to help them, but they are struggling with the massive amount of misinformation available through the Internet and other sources. Parents seeking treatment for children with trauma and attachment disorders need understanding, validation, and solutions.

HOW TO USE THIS BOOK

If you are a parent, we suggest you use this guide in conjunction with therapeutic help. For your child and family to readily change and heal, work must be done both at home and in therapy. This guide, along with your therapeutic team, will help you develop a deeper understanding of your traumatized child and help you learn and implement specific skills that will help change your child's brain.

There is an overwhelming amount of advice available to parents about disciplining children, and there is a tremendous amount of confusing and conflicting information available related to attachment. Here you will find clear, consistent information and learn how early trauma and loss have impacted your child's thoughts, feelings, and behaviors.

The first chapter addresses your child's brain and the neurological impact of attachment trauma. As you begin to understand the profound effects of your child's adverse early experiences on his or her neurological functioning, emotional security, and capacity to trust, you may discover a paradigm shift in your thoughts about, and emotional responses to your child. It is easy to fall into the common misperception that aggressive and defiant behaviors are motivated by rage and intentional desire to manipulate. Through the information in this guide, you will come to understand the connection between your child's behaviors and the store of traumatic experiences in his or her brain—and you will likely no longer assume rage and manipulation as motivators.

In the second chapter you will learn that there are effective ways to approach your child that can help increase his or her ability to manage and tolerate feelings. As you explore the practice of mindfulness, you will learn to attune to your child's deeper feelings and strengthen his or her sense of security and trust so your child can heal at an emotional level. Once a true emotional connection has been made, you will discover greater success in helping your child behave more appropriately.

Chapter 2 also educates you on how to bring joy, laughter, and play back into your home. Shared pleasure, play, and fun will enable you and your child to feel connected, thus strengthening his or her security with you. You will learn how trauma impacts play and discover tips for helping your child heal through healthy play.

Chapter 3 provides a way of understanding major meltdowns and how to manage them. There are phases and characteristics of meltdowns, as well as specific skills to manage each phase. Chapter 3 also addresses other challenging behaviors such as lying, stealing, aggression, defiance, and sexualized behaviors. You will learn tips that will help you manage these behaviors in a more attuned way, while building and strengthening the relationship.

Of course, you are important, too. In Chapter 4 you will learn about your own triggers and feelings and how to take better care of yourself. Learning the intricacies of your emotions and perceptions about yourself and your relationship with your child are key components in dealing with difficult ongoing behaviors. Gaining insight into your own meltdowns will help you become more aware and enhance your ability to make changes in your reactions and responses to your child.

In the last chapter you will learn strategies and consider suggestions for managing tricky day-to-day behaviors and giving appropriate consequences. The word *discipline* means "to teach." Helping your child gain insight into cause-and-effect relationships will help him or her to link personal choices to outcomes/consequences. Understanding cause-and-effect actions and shaping what happens next are critical components on the journey to healing and to leading a safe, healthy life. This chapter will help you rethink how and when to give consequences and how to reward positive behaviors effectively.

This guide accompanies the clinician's treatment book, *Integrative Team Treatment for Attachment Trauma in Children: Family Therapy and EMDR* (Wesselmann, Schweitzer, & Armstrong, 2014). The material in this book will serve as a reference during your child's family therapy sessions. It is essential learning, a foundation for discussion, and a resource.

Parenting is the most difficult and the most important job in the world. You may find the *Integrative Parenting* methods taught in these pages to be very different from other approaches with which you are familiar. Like anything new, there is a learning curve—but please, keep an open mind, and give these new methods a try. In conjunction with ongoing support from your child's therapeutic team, we believe you will find that the *Integrative Parenting* strategies will open doors to deeper connections and greater happiness within your family.

INTEGRATIVE
PARENTING

Chapter 1

Scared Children, Not Scary Children

By the conclusion of this first chapter, you will be able to . . .

1. Identify the traumatic events in your child's early life.
2. Identify the negative core beliefs driving your child's challenging behaviors and blocking his or her success. Identify when your child is operating outside of his or her "window of tolerance" (Siegel, 2010).
3. Recognize the triggers to your child's concerning behaviors.
4. Understand the rationale for the use of EMDR (eye movement desensitization and reprocessing) and family therapy to treat your child, and learn how you can support and participate in the therapy.

YOU ARE NOT ALONE

If you are a parent reading this book, you are probably struggling in your relationship with your child—whether your child came to your family through adoption, guardianship, foster care, or through birth, and whether your child is a planned or a completely unplanned part of your life. This book accompanies a treatment book for therapists entitled *Integrative Team Treatment for Attachment Trauma in Children: Family Therapy and EMDR* (Wesselmann, Schweitzer, & Armstrong, 2014). You may be participating, or considering participation, in the therapeutic approach that it describes. Your child's therapeutic team may include a psychiatrist or occupational therapist in addition to a family therapist and EMDR therapist. We will talk more about your child's therapy later in this chapter. This guide is designed not just to help you manage your child's behaviors at home while you are involved in this therapy, but to assist you in becoming an integral part of your child's therapeutic "team." Because your child's ability to feel secure within his or her attachment relationships has been damaged, your role in your child's healing process is vital.

Parents' Emotions

The parents who bring their children to our facility for treatment have many intense feelings, but the feeling underlying all the others is *fear*. Indeed, the behaviors of children with a history of attachment trauma can be frightening. Their actions can be shocking and startling to parents, grandparents, aunts, uncles, teachers, counselors, doctors, and others. These children sometimes exhibit aggressive and frightening behaviors in the home, but outside of the home appear calm and cooperative. In this situation, parents are often reluctant to ask for help because they fear that the professionals will blame them or will not believe them.

You may find your heart racing during your child's meltdowns. You may feel anxious and overwhelmed because your child threatens you or hits, bites, and kicks. You may lie awake at night wondering what will happen to your child when he is old enough to go to jail for stealing. You may fear that he will someday become a sexual predator due to his sexualized behaviors at his young age. Your fear may lead you to do things that resemble your child's actions—you may find yourself screaming, yelling, hitting, or slamming things. Afterwards, you may find yourself overwhelmed with guilt and shame.

You are emotionally invested in your child and his welfare, yet you may feel utterly powerless to help him. You are probably completely confused as to why your child acts the way she does. You are not alone. Your struggles are shared by thousands of other parents raising hurt children. We have written this parent guide because you are an important part of your child's supportive "team." This book will help you (1) to understand the memories, emotions, and beliefs that drive your child's present-day behaviors; (2) to implement *Integrative Parenting* strategies designed to help your child's brain function better so that he can more easily change his thoughts and feelings; and (3) to enhance the success of your child's treatment. We believe that you will feel less afraid and more and more empowered as you read through the pages of this book. When you learn about the traumatic roots to your child's behavioral problems, we believe that you will better understand your "scary" child as a "scared" child.

Repairing the Bond as Guardians or Adoptive or Foster Parents

You may be a foster parent, a guardian, or an adoptive parent. You may or may not be a biological relative to the child in your care. In any of these situations, your child's first attachment was not with you. Your child may have been with her biological parents for a few hours or a few years. Her experience with these biological parents may have been wonderful for a short time, until one or both parents suddenly disappeared from her life—or it may have been stressful from the start. Your child may have repeatedly experienced hunger, pain, loneliness, or fear due to family circumstances involving emotional illness, drugs and alcohol abuse, domestic abuse, poverty, or other stressors. Your child may have experienced orphanage care or foster care where there were many strange faces and no consistent person with whom to bond.

As you begin reading this guide, you will come to understand how your child's present-day behaviors and relationships have been affected by his earlier life experiences. Although you and your child are participating in family therapy and EMDR with professionals, the last four chapters of this book will help *you* also become an agent of change. You will learn to implement *Integrative Parenting* strategies to promote healthy attachment and healthy behaviors.

Repairing the Bond as the Biological Parent

You may be reading this book as a biological parent to a child who was traumatized in his early life. You may have been separated from your child due to his illness, your illness, deployment, divorce, or problems that you had with an addiction. You yourself may have frightened or hurt your child due to emotional problems or substance abuse problems with which you were dealing. Or your child may have experienced some kind of physical or emotional neglect or abuse or frightening circumstances in whatever place he was living. If you have worked on fixing your own situation and now you are trying to renew a relationship with your child, you may be facing tremendous challenges, but with the help of your child's therapeutic team and this guide, you can change the stuck patterns of interactions in your home and heal your relationship with your child.

WHAT IS *ATTACHMENT* ANYWAY?

Attachment is an inborn survival mechanism, designed by nature. Infants and children who fall in love with their parents yearn to be with them, and this attachment allows them to survive their first several years on the planet. Parents are also designed to fall in love and bond with their infants, and their strong desire to be with them ensures that the infants are nurtured and kept safe. When parents meet both the emotional and physical needs of their children, their children develop more than just a generic attachment. They are categorized as having a "secure" attachment—an overall trusting outlook that carries over and enhances other relationships later on and creates a general sense of safety in the world.

Alternatives to a Secure Attachment

Your child may not have had the opportunity to develop a healthy attachment to anyone as an infant. If she was placed immediately into orphanage care or moved from home to home in foster care, she may have been "unattached" for a period of time, which means that she may need to be patiently coached into a relationship with you. However, if your child spent any amount of time with a parent or caregiver, she may have had a "falling in love" experience of attachment with that person. She may have formed an attachment to a parent or someone else who then disappeared from her life, leaving her bereft and unable to trust anyone again. She may have developed an "anxious" type of attachment, because her first parent was depressed, preoccupied, overwhelmed, or substance abusing, or she may have developed what is called a "disorganized" attachment because she was afraid of her parent. Fear experienced in response to the parent creates disorganization in the child's thoughts, emotions, and behaviors.

The influence of attachment experiences on lifelong perceptions and behaviors was not fully recognized until the latter half of the twentieth century. Read about the early development of attachment theory in Text Box 1.1.

THE INGREDIENTS OF SECURE ATTACHMENT

In our view, there are four critical components: touch and eye contact, emotional attunement, a secure holding environment, and shared pleasure, play, and fun. Parents must provide these critical components to help their children develop an attachment that is healthy and secure. Children continue to need these ingredients of secure attachment until they grow up and launch new adult relationships. Your child probably became anxious or disorganized if the four critical components were not met for a significant span of time, whether it was during infancy, toddlerhood, or later childhood. Security can become insecurity when a stable early environment turns into a chaotic one later on.

Box 1.1. Gray Matter: Origins of Attachment Theory

John Bowlby was a 20th-century psychiatrist and researcher in England who conceptualized attachment theory. Bowlby studied young children who were separated from their parents for long periods of time due to the war or for medical reasons. He observed that the children exhibited three stages of grief over the separations; (1) angry protest, (2) despair, and (3) withdrawal/apathy. After reunification with the parents, however, he noted lasting effects in the children's ability to trust and be close. Later researchers observed mother and infant pairs and found that when mothers are not emotionally sensitive to their babies' needs, the babies exhibit definite signs of insecurity. Babies and toddlers of mothers who are abusive or affected by unresolved losses and traumas exhibit the most concerning behaviors and are categorized "disorganized." Bowlby concluded that we are wired from birth to attach to our parents, because staying close to them helps us survive. By the same token, attachment separations, inconsistent care, or mistreatment can lead to long-term insecurity and mistrust (Ainsworth, 1982; Bowlby, 1973; Main & Solomon, 1990).

Touch and Eye Contact

In ideal circumstances, touch and eye contact begin at birth. When parents are not overwhelmed by stress, mental illness, or other outside forces, they are naturally drawn to holding and gazing at their newborns. Love hormones, called *opioids*, flood the brain of both the baby and the parents, creating a wonderful "falling-in-love" feeling. In such ideal circumstances, babies grow to love the sensations of touch, and the parents grow to love the feeling of being with their child. When their babies cry, parents who are emotionally present feel an urgent need to comfort them so that they can feel that good feeling again. By doing so, the babies feel better and so do the parents. As children grow older, they continue to need touch. Physical affection, conversation, and eye contact help children feel significant and connected to their parents.

Think about the barriers that may have existed to physical touch in your child's earlier experiences. There may have been circumstances causing physical separation, such as hospitalization (of the child or yourself), divorce, imprisonment, or deployment. Your child may have had a parent who was emotionally overwhelmed by poverty, trauma, losses, mental illness, relationship conflicts, domestic violence, alcoholism or drug addiction, or a too-young parent who was not developmentally ready to have a child. Your child's parent may have learned parenting behaviors that were passed down generation to generation. Your child may have had to shut down his needs for touch in order to cope, or he may have become demanding of attention in an attempt to overcome his loneliness.

Emotional Attunement

In optimal circumstances, happy, calm parents think a great deal about the inner experience of their children. Parents make guesses: He is hungry. He seems overly tired. He is bored. She is lonely. When parents read the cues of their children and accurately interpret their facial expressions, their cries, or their actions and respond to these needs, children sense their parents' concern and learn to trust their parents to give them what they need. If parents' circumstances allow them to observe, listen, and think about their children's feelings and needs, then their children develop a sense of self and awareness of their own feelings. When attuned parents reassure and calm their upset children, their children begin internalizing their parents' reassuring words and learn to calm themselves.

There are some other important by-products of having emotionally attuned parents. Children who are raised by emotionally attuned parents learn to be unafraid of their own emotions, because their parents respond in a caring way, without getting upset. These children learn how to verbally express their emotions, because they know their parents will listen. Over time, they become good at coping with adversity, because their parents help them think and problem-solve.

Consider your child's earlier life. Has your child always had someone in his life who was emotionally attuned and sensitively responsive to his needs? When parents are emotionally overwhelmed by their own circumstances, provision of food and shelter may be the best they can do. Parents who are "just surviving" are usually unable to take the time to "tune in" to their children emotionally or provide needed comfort. Your child's emotional and even physical needs may have been forgotten for a significant period of time, leaving him anxious and emotionally alone.

The Secure Holding Environment

Children need to be free of worry about their own safety, about getting fed, and about the behavior of the significant adults in their lives (unpredictable behavior is unhealthy). The "secure holding environment" is a term coined by Donald Winnicott (1987), an English psychiatrist, who used this term to describe the safe, predictable, nurturing environment ideally provided by parents after a child is born. The secure holding environment is required for children to relax, trust, open up emotionally, and experience a sense of security with their parents. Your child may have experienced attachment insecurity and a high level of anxiety due to chaos in her earlier environment. She may have learned to cope by acting out her anxiety or by shutting down, or both.

Shared Pleasure, Play, and Fun

Parents who are happy and secure are playful. When parents are happy, they naturally strive to make their youngsters happy. When parents and their children share fun and play, opioids are released in the brain, the parents and children feel closer, and the children learn healthy ways to "light up" the pleasure circuits in their own brains.

Did your child lack the opportunity to experience shared joy and play for a significant time in his earlier life? His earlier caregivers may have experienced parenthood as more stressful than pleasurable. Overwhelmed parents typically lack the desire to play or have fun with their children. Parents who are severely depressed are unable to enjoy their child and play. The idea of play may be foreign to parents who grew up in a deprived environment.

Your child may have missed out on some of the important ingredients of a positive attachment experience in the very first part of his life, or he may have received sensitive, nurturing care in the beginning, followed by more difficult times later. If your child did not experience adequate touch, emotional attunement, safety, and play for a significant period at any point in his young life, then his ability to trust and feel connected has been greatly compromised.

NURTURING THE INTEGRATED BRAIN

You may be familiar with the description of the individual who is "right-brain dominant" as someone who is emotional, creative, and artistic. An individual who is more logical and less emotional is often described as "left-brain dominant." In general, the right hemisphere is the seat of emotions and creativity, whereas the left hemisphere is the location of rational, logical thought.

At birth, we are feelers, not thinkers; the left brain is not yet operational. Optimally, *Integrative Parenting* begins at birth. As infants attach and parents bond, the baby is soothed again and again. Schore (1996) explains that the baby's brain and the parent's brain harmonize, and over time, the baby's brain actually organizes itself to replicate the parent's brain. In this way, nurturing a baby actually promotes healthy brain growth.

One important region that does not develop to its potential without the help of a nurturing parent is called the *prefrontal cortex*. This region is located just behind the baby's eyes, and is responsible for focus and concentration, sound decision-making, frustration tolerance, empathy, and the ability to shift from one focus to another. Siegel and Bryson (2011) explain that the prefrontal region is also vital to neurological integration because it is positioned to link all the major regions of the brain. A well-developed prefrontal brain allows the thinking upper cortex to link with the emotional center of the brain, and also with the brainstem below, which is responsible for basic bodily functions. If you examine the brain in terms of the right and left hemispheres, it is clear that the prefrontal brain region also spans the two halves of the brain. As parents emotionally attune to their children, they are nurturing prefrontal brain development and brain integration, giving their children the capacity to feel and think logically at the same time. This kind of integrated brain functioning leads to increased coping, better problem-solving, and more creative thinking.

Your child may have missed out on some of the healthy ingredients of attachment security during the first few months or years of life, so she did not experience optimal prefrontal brain growth and integration between the two hemispheres. By implementing *Integrative Parenting* strategies and participating in the Integrative Team Treatment approach with your child, you will be helping your child develop communication between the right and left hemispheres. You will be working toward improved neurological functioning and calming of your child's brain, in addition to changing your child's beliefs and feelings. This is not a quick fix, but it *is* possible, through the combined efforts of your child's therapeutic team and you.

HOW EARLIER EXPERIENCES CHANGED YOUR CHILD'S MOST IMPORTANT BELIEFS

Your child's earlier experiences taught him how to think about himself, others, and the world in general. Throughout childhood and even into adulthood, a child's core belief system tends to remain unshakable, unless someone intervenes in a meaningful way.

The Optimal Belief System

The infant who feels safe, loved, and nurtured learns that others are looking out for him. The child will naturally lean toward a positive interpretation of the behaviors of others, and he will probably have an optimistic outlook on life. In general, *the child who is nurtured and protected will believe . . .*

- "I can trust that my parents always love me."
- "I can trust my parents to be in charge and take good care of me."
- "I can ask for help."
- "It's safe to be vulnerable."
- "It's safe to love and trust."
- "I'm loved and lovable, and I don't have to be perfect."
- "I belong."
- "I'm good and I deserve good things."
- "The world is generally a good place."
- "I can expect good things from others."

The child who holds these positive beliefs naturally turns to his parents for comfort, enjoys closeness, and trusts his parents to be in charge. He feels relaxed, eager to explore his relationships and his world, and experiences pleasure from day-to-day life. The child with a positive belief system seeks out enjoyable relationships later on and is drawn to adulthood relationships that match his earlier positive relationship experiences.

The Negative Belief System

Your child may have lived in a chaotic, stressful, or even frightening environment for a lengthy period of time at some point before she came to live with you. She may have felt anxious or fearful, even with her caregivers. She may have felt close to a caregiver who then vanished, leaving her feeling bereft and alone. Your child may have been with you during a period when your life was out of control, or when she had a painful medical condition that was not easily fixed; or she may have been separated from you for a lengthy period of time for some reason.

Experiences that were sad or frightening for your child most likely led to anxious and negative beliefs. These beliefs may have actually been true at one point, even if they are no longer true. However, just as someone walking around indoors unknowingly wearing dark glasses is certain that the room is dim and dark, the child with a negative belief system has no idea that he is impaired. He doesn't know that his negative beliefs are coloring his interpretations of the events around him and causing him to react in an illogical manner.

If your child felt unsafe, unloved, or alone over a lengthy period of time, he or she may have learned to believe:

- "There is no one to help me."
- "It's not safe to trust my parents to care about what I need."
- "I'm not important."
- "I can't get what I need."
- "I'm not safe."
- "I can't get the closeness and love I need."
- "It's not safe to have needs or feelings."
- "I'm not good enough."
- "I'm a mistake."
- "It's not safe to love."
- "I'm all alone."
- "There is no one to whom I can go for comfort."
- "Bad things will happen."
- "I will always be rejected and abandoned."
- "Parents are mean."
- "Parents leave."
- "I don't belong anywhere."
- "It's not safe to trust or get close."

The human race is designed for survival, no matter the quality of the life. In order to survive in a world where these things are true, children make some rules for themselves that allow them to survive in a world that feels unsafe. These survival rules become part of their core belief system and stick with them—even when their environment becomes safe and the present family is nurturing. Think about your child's behaviors and hypothesize which of these survival rules he or she may have adopted.

Common survival rules include . . .

- "I must take care of getting my own needs met by myself, in any way I can."
- "I must take what I need/want whenever I have the chance." (A child, of course, cannot distinguish between what he or she *wants* and what he or she truly *needs*.)
- "I must cry and demand so that you will see me and hear me."
- "I must keep a wall up and not care about others, so I will not get hurt."
- "I must be vigilant to danger and mistrust others at all times."
- "I must stay in control of my environment in order to stay safe."
- "I must not allow myself to be open or vulnerable in any way."
- "I must fight to defend myself at all costs."
- "I must be ready to run to survive."
- "I must be ready to freeze, hide, or close up to protect myself."

Even though you are trustworthy and well meaning, your child's learned beliefs obscure the truth about you. His beliefs prevent him from accepting and enjoying your love and affection. This does not mean that he does not want love and closeness; deep down, he wants your love and affection very much. He doesn't know how to accept love and remain safe, so he demands attention one minute, and pushes you away the next.

Your child may be on a challenging life trajectory. His social development may be delayed because his vigilance to danger and need to be in control prevent him from developing close relationships and having fun. His education may be suffering because his vigilance and intense emotions prevent him from focusing properly in school. His emotional development may lag behind other children his own age because no one helped him with his emotions in his earlier life, and now he does not know how to go to you for comfort or assistance when he is stressed or distressed. Instead, he pushes his emotions away by acting out.

Put on Your "Detective's Hat"

In therapy sessions, your child's therapist will frequently encourage both you and your child to "put on the detective's hat." We encourage parents to become part of our "team" as we look for clues regarding the child's belief system. You can begin this process now, at home.

Don't try to figure out your child's core beliefs by asking her. Your child does not have the maturity and insight she needs to critically examine her own thinking. You can develop a good hypothesis about her beliefs by thinking about what she may have learned from her past, and by observing her present-day behaviors.

For example, if your child was neglected for a period of time and now takes things without asking, she developed the logical belief, "It's not safe to trust my parents to care about what I need." She now follows the survival rule: "I must be in charge of getting what I need." If your child was abused on multiple occasions and now vacillates between pushing you away and pulling you close, she probably learned, "I can't trust." She follows the survival rules, "I must be vigilant to danger. I must not allow myself to be vulnerable and open. I must keep a wall around myself."

Accurate identification of your child's negative beliefs and survival rules is a critical component of EMDR (see the section at the end of this chapter) and to *Integrative Parenting*. The following transcript illustrates a family therapy session in which the therapist is meeting with Tom's mother, prior to bringing Tom into the session. Mom and Tom's therapist identify some of Tom's negative beliefs during this meeting.

Mom: I'm so frustrated. Tom consistently lies to me whenever I observe that he has either done something he shouldn't have, or he has forgotten to do something he should have. His lies are rambling and incoherent. They don't even make sense.

Family Therapist: It's clear that he becomes extremely anxious as soon as he realizes he has been "caught" in a mistake. Let's think about beliefs Tom may have developed during his earlier life experiences that may be driving this behavior.

Mom: Well, I know that he was removed from his biological family because of harsh physical abuse by his biological dad. I'm sure he was probably physically punished whenever he did something wrong.

Family Therapist: That fits, doesn't it? He must hold a negative belief related to making a mistake.

Mom: Well, sure, he must believe it isn't safe to make a mistake. He probably believes he is bad and that he will be hurt if he makes a mistake of some kind.

Family Therapist: So, "I'm bad if I make a mistake" and "I'm in danger if I make a mistake." Do you think those beliefs fit?

Mom: Yes, that's it. And so he follows the survival rule, "Don't admit to a mistake no matter what." That totally explains this behavior.

UNDERSTANDING YOUR CHILD THROUGH THE TRAUMA LENS

We all experience a variety of emotions in our lives. We have a built-in "information processing" system, which means that we naturally work through our emotions, consciously and subconsciously, on a daily basis. We process much of our emotional baggage from the day during the REM (rapid eye movement) stage of sleep.

Francine Shapiro (2007), originator of EMDR (a trauma treatment described later in this chapter), explains that a traumatic event can overload our natural information processing system. The system shuts down and the traumatic event is stored in an unprocessed form. Flashes of pictures from the event plus emotions, body sensations, and beliefs associated with the event are all stored within a separate neural network in the emotional center, or limbic region, of the brain. Any reminder of the trauma can tap right into the stored material, flooding us with upsetting feelings, images, or sensations, sometimes with no conscious insight as to why we are feeling what we are feeling.

Your child may have a large store of traumatic memories. Present-day situations that either consciously or subconsciously remind your child of earlier traumatic events naturally tap into his earlier emotions and sensations. Although your child's responses to present-day situations frequently appear irrational, those same responses might seem logical if you had a window through which you could see into your child's traumatic past.

What Is Attachment Trauma?

We think of attachment trauma as any traumatic past experience associated with attachment figures that damages children's ability to feel safe and secure within their primary relationships. Attachment trauma is particularly damaging because children are supposed to feel safe and protected by their parental figures. When the very person to whom the child wishes to run is at the same time the source of the child's fear or distress, he or she is left in an intolerable position. Children do not have the emotional resources with which to cope with life on their own. When the parent is the source of their emotional pain, there is no way out for them.

Early "Big T" Traumas

Shapiro (2007, 2012) uses the terms "Big T" trauma and "small t" trauma to differentiate between traumatic events that are dangerous, physically painful, or life-threatening from those that are distressing, but not truly dangerous. Your child may have experienced "Big T" trauma associated with physical or sexual assault, going hungry, witnessing domestic violence, or other frightening behaviors on the part of parents or others.

Sometimes circumstances that cannot be prevented lead to "Big T" traumas. Infants and young children undergoing painful illnesses or medical interventions may not understand that their parents are trying to help but cannot remove the pain. They may perceive that the adults are causing the pain or that no one cares about their pain. An adolescent girl we treated had developed the belief that her mother was mean. She had endured extensive painful surgeries during her first few years of life, and after each surgery, the first thing she saw was her mother's face. Her mother's face had become associated with the pain and confusion.

"Big T" traumas for children may include:

- Physical or sexual assault by a parent or another person who is older and stronger
- Going hungry
- Being left alone
- Witnessing violence
- Witnessing frightening behaviors in adults who are mentally ill or abusing substances
- Early painful illnesses or medical interventions
- Sudden loss of a parent

Early "small t" Traumas

Events that do not create a fear of death can still be traumatic because they diminish the child's sense of significance and worth or create a sense of being unloved and alone. A sense of being alone, rejected, confused, ashamed, or worthless can leave a child in terrible despair. This type of experience is called "small t" trauma, only because the event does not cause threat of physical harm. However, these experiences are distressing enough that they can overwhelm the child's natural information processing system, leaving the memories stored in an unprocessed form.

In addition to loss of caregivers, orphanage and foster care, molestation, or rejection, feelings of desolation and abandonment can result from medical experiences that no one could have prevented. Often children have felt emotional abandonment by parents who truly do love them, but whose circumstances have simply led to an inability to function properly.

Examples of "small t" traumas include:

• Moved from caregiver to caregiver
• Orphanage care
• Hospitalization
• Mother's hospitalization and/or serious physical illness
• Ridicule/rejection/emotional abuse

Preverbal Trauma

Years ago, it was believed that events experienced by children who were too young to remember had no impact on them. Now, scientists and child experts know differently. Like other traumatic events, the memories of the emotions and body sensations associated with neglect, abuse, abandonment, or medical trauma experienced in the first 2 years of life are stored in the emotional, or limbic, region of the brain. Although few of us can consciously recall much if anything prior to age 2, the feelings associated with any preverbal trauma are still within us. Reminders of the preverbal events won't help us find the memory consciously, but they may trigger associated emotions and sensations, even if we don't understand their source. Many children suffering from attachment trauma carry early trauma stored in the limbic brain, and they are unable to consciously recall or describe the memories, even though the early events may be driving their emotional reactions and behaviors. Luckily, it is not necessary for children to "recall" these early events in order to heal. With patience and the right tools, therapists and parents can help their children "heal" from trauma experienced during infancy.

HYPERAROUSAL AND HYPOAROUSAL

Our brains are designed to be aware of dangerous circumstances and to help us respond in the most self-protective way possible. When the brain becomes "aroused" or alert in response to real or imagined danger, there are a variety of ways in which it can cue the body to respond. Read Text Box 1.2 to learn how the varying responses to threat are related to the evolution of our species.

Box 1.2. Gray Matter: The Survival Brain

Researcher Stephen Porges (2011) explains that as the human brain has evolved, the vagal nerves have developed the capacity to activate the brain to respond to threat in various ways. The most primitive response is the "vegetative vagal" response, which activates the parasympathetic nervous system, slowing respiration and heart rate. This "shut down" mode is reminiscent of the way a lizard or an opossum might freeze and "play dead" at the sight of a hawk overhead. The "mammalian" vagal nerve response, which developed later in the brain's evolutionary development, activates the sympathetic nervous system. The increased heart and respiration rates ready an individual for action, in the way a rabbit becomes instantly aroused and ready to bolt for safety or a wolf springs into action when it smells an enemy. The most advanced evolutionary vagal nerve response to threat is the response of communication and negotiation. The child who can calmly talk his or her way out of trouble reads social cues and uses communication in a way that only human beings can. Typically, children impacted by attachment trauma lack this more advanced communication response, because their brains were wired for survival responses before they had the ability to speak—thus, only the more primitive responses are available to them. The activation of the fight, flight, freeze, or shut-down response pattern is reflexive (i.e., it occurs automatically) when there is a perception of threat (Porges, 2011).

Hyperarousal

The limbic region, or emotional center, of the brain is in charge of releasing stress hormones into the brain if danger is detected. When any of us feels threatened, the stress hormones help us prepare to fight or run away by increasing our heart rate and respiration, or we hold our body very still, ready to spring into action. Digestion of food is also stopped, allowing our body to put all its energy into running or fighting the enemy. This is "Mother Nature" giving us the equipment to go to battle when needed. If your child felt unsafe for a significant period of time in his life, he is probably wired to remain in a state of *hyperarousal*. In hyperarousal, he may argue, throw fits, or act out in other ways; he may run away or freeze and hide while remaining tense and ready to spring into action.

Hypoarousal

Hypoarousal is the opposite of hyperarousal. We have all experienced the hypoaroused state when we can no longer concentrate on a boring lecture, or we are waiting in a long line and we "go away" mentally or "space out." Our heart rate and respiration actually slow down, and we may not even be aware of the passage of time.

Hypoarousal is also another response to perceived danger when it appears that there is no way out of a situation. In response to threat hypoarousal appears to be associated with "giving up." Another word for this is *dissociation*. Infants and young children are most likely to dissociate when they are in danger because there is no way for them to fight or run. If your child lived with fear for a period of time as an infant or very young child, he probably experienced frequent hypoarousal, and he may now be wired to dissociate whenever he is stressed. Dissociation can become an unhealthy way of coping with anything difficult that comes along. Many children vacillate between hyperarousal and hypoarousal. One minute your child may be anxious or aggressive, and the next he may be shut down.

THE WINDOW OF TOLERANCE

Figure 1.1 illustrates a concept adapted from Ogden and Minton (2000) and the work of Daniel Siegel (2010) that pertains to each one of us and is especially helpful for understanding the mental state of children with a history of attachment trauma. Every one of us has a different tolerance for emotions, and we all cope better some days than other days. Our *window of tolerance* represents the amount of distress we can endure and still remain calm on a particular day. When we are experiencing distress that we can tolerate, we remain within the window that is represented by the box in the center of Figure 1.1. Although we may be experiencing some level of anxiety or other disturbing emotion, we continue to function normally. Within our tolerance level for distress, we can still enjoy love and caring for friends and family. We can still receive comfort and affection, comprehend and remember new information, and communicate with others.

If our distress level becomes unmanageable, we move outside of our relatively calm window and lose the capacity to think rationally, problem-solve, or express ourselves. We lose the ability to give and receive affection, to feel connected, or to

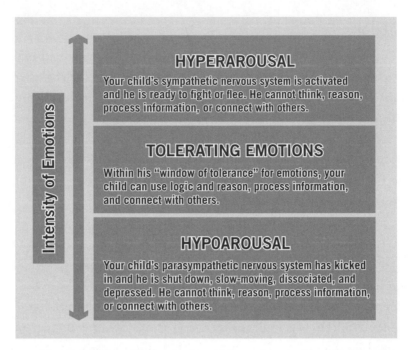

FIGURE 1.1. The window of tolerance, adapted from the works of Ogden and Minton (2000) and Siegel (2010), is a visual representation of the limits of emotional intensity a child (or adult) can tolerate without losing the ability to think logically, learn, and socialize.

learn and remember things. Most of us have experienced this state of mind in brief bursts from time to time—after a near miss in traffic . . . while running to catch a flight . . . or perhaps while taking an important exam. Some of us have experienced longer periods of overwhelming distress in which we struggled with impatience, short-term memory loss, inability to make decisions, and impulsivity.

Children who have received physical affection and emotional attunement from parents in a secure, safe environment develop a wide window of tolerance for distress. They have learned not to be afraid of their own feelings, but to verbalize them. They have internalized their parents' reassuring words and developed the ability to calm themselves, and they have learned to trust that their parents will protect them and help them, no matter what. Because of this foundation of trust, external stressors do not easily overwhelm them. They can feel and express their feelings, calm themselves, and they can still learn and socialize effectively in school and elsewhere.

Your child, on the other hand, may have only a very narrow window of tolerance for distress. For a significant time during her development, she may have had no one to help her express her feelings, problem-solve, or calm down. In general, she may not believe that the world and relationships are safe. She may not trust herself to solve problems or manage stress, and she has no faith that she can depend on others to assist her. She may live with ongoing levels of underlying anxiety. Your child may be unable to manage even minute levels of additional distress, and subsequently, she may spend inordinate amounts of time outside of her window.

Your child may become triggered into a state of hyperarousal, represented by the upper window in Figure 1.1, on most days. In the hyperaroused state, her heart rate and respiration are high. Her thinking brain is "offline" while the emotional region of her brain is activated, so she regularly struggles with learning, communicating logically, developing relationships, and solving problems. Signs of hyperarousal may include arguing, defiance, stealing, lying, hoarding, overeating, guardedness, excessive talking, trouble focusing or concentrating, sexual acting out, "attitude," reactivity, difficulty sleeping, and nightmares.

If your child is frequently triggered and stressed, she may frequently shift to a state of hypoarousal (the lower window in Figure 1.1). Your child may be predisposed towards hypoarousal if she experienced a high level of distress in infancy. In hypoarousal, like hyperarousal, socializing or learning are pretty much impossible. Signs of hypoarousal may include looking "spaced out," shut down, or quiet, slow in movement or speech, clumsy, and unable to focus or concentrate.

Children who spend a great amount of time in either hyper- or hypoaroused states need our help to expand their window of tolerance for distress. They also need help to increase their sense of safety and connection with their parents and to manage their triggers. The parenting tools described in this book, along with your child's therapeutic team, will help your child widen his or her window, given time and patience.

IDENTIFYING YOUR CHILD'S TRIGGERS

When early trauma is associated with parents or caregivers, the negative feelings and beliefs are thereafter triggered by parent figures in all sorts of ways. Parent figures are associated with fear, anxiety, hurt, mistrust, and feelings of rejection and worthlessness. Due to your child's earlier attachment traumas, she may be unable to view you as a source of safety and security. Attempts to parent her may trigger her mistrust. Your child may be triggered by teachers and classmates as well. She may be triggered into hyperarousal or hypoarousal by a myriad of events and situations.

Deep down, your child desperately wants love and affection. She does not trust affection or nurturing because she is certain that she will ultimately be rejected or abandoned. You may feel like a yo-yo as your child pulls you close and then pushes you away, over and over again!

If your child believes that it is not safe to love you, to let you be in charge, or to receive affection from you, then your child may be triggered to fight (argue, hit, kick, meltdown), flee (run off, disappear), freeze (stiffen), or dissociate (shut down, become spacey) whenever you attempt to . . .

- Say "no," ask her to do something, or redirect her.
- Attempt to give her physical affection.
- Attempt to praise her or give verbal affection.

If your child was traumatized by loss, abuse, or neglect, she may be extremely sensitive to "alone" feelings, which are sometimes described as "bored." She may have great difficulty trusting that she is loved and that she belongs, and she is easily triggered to feel "insignificant" and "unloved" by separations or parents' business with other things.

If your child holds negative beliefs that he is unloved, he doesn't belong, or he is alone, he may be triggered to fight, flee, freeze, or shut down when you attempt to . . .

- Send him to his room.
- Talk on the phone.
- Visit with your partner or a friend.
- Pay attention to a sibling.

If your child felt rejected earlier in his life, he may believe that he caused the rejection by his own defectiveness. He may view mistakes and misbehaviors as evidence that he truly is bad and utterly worthless at the core. He may feel driven to hide the deep, dark secret of his "badness" by overreacting with defensiveness whenever he is redirected. This defensive mode may trigger your child to fight, flee, freeze, or shut down when you attempt to . . .

- Call attention to a misbehavior.
- Question your child.
- Give a redirection.

If your child was not given what she needed when she was hungry, thirsty, wet, lonely, or afraid, she may be unable to relax and trust you to provide for her, make decisions for her, or even comfort her. Out of an innate drive to survive, she may feel the need to be in charge of getting her own needs met by crying, whining, demanding, sneaking, hoarding, or stealing. She won't ask you for what she needs, and she may not be able to go to you for comfort or support. It literally does not occur to her to do so. She may be triggered to seek what she needs in any way she can when she has a desire for something, or when she feels hungry, lonely, or afraid. She has "needs" and "wants" all mixed up. Everything feels equally important to her, and the sneaking, stealing, and demanding behaviors may be triggered by . . .

- The sight of something enticing
- Hunger
- Loneliness
- Fear

If your child lives in a highly anxious state, she may constantly look for something to self-soothe. This seeking behavior is not a conscious activity, but quite automatic for any child living with high levels of anxiety. Your child may become very controlling and demanding of attention in order to feel better, or she may seek comfort through other means. She may turn to sexualized ways of feeling good, comfort foods that are sweet or salty, or obsessive use of video games. If she is an adolescent, she is at risk for use of substances to feel better.

PARENTS' TRIGGERS

Children with behaviors associated with attachment trauma learn to mistrust early in life. Unfortunately, their behaviors are extremely provocative and challenging and frequently trigger extreme feelings in their parents, who are trying to help them. You are only human, and you may feel rejected, hurt, anxious, mistrusting, and resentful. You may develop your own set of negative beliefs related to your child and yourself, including:

- "My child dislikes me."
- "My child wants to hurt me."
- "My child is evil/bad/shameful."
- "My child is an embarrassment to me."
- "I'm a bad parent."
- "I'm not in control."
- "This is hopeless."

Practice noticing when you have these negative thoughts and pick up this book and read the following statements to yourself. Remind yourself that these are the facts:

- "My child is not bad—he has a narrow window of tolerance and he needs my help to widen it."
- "Even though I am a target when my child acts out, his behavior stems from his survival brain and really has nothing to do with me."
- "With therapy and *Integrative Parenting* strategies, over time, I can help my child develop trust, expand his window, and calm his brain."
- "I can improve my child's future and our future relationship by investing the time and energy today."

You may have run across out-of-date information on the Internet that has been disturbing or frightening to you. Text Box 1.3 describes the old way and the new way of understanding children who struggle with a traumatic past, to assist you in discerning fact from fiction.

YOUR CHILD'S THERAPY

Your child's prefrontal brain may not have developed optimally in earlier life. However, you and your child's therapeutic team can help promote prefrontal growth and brain integration through *Integrative Parenting* strategies. The human brain can grow new neurons and neural connections in response to positive environmental changes, even into adulthood and old age. This phenomenon, called *neural plasticity*, means that we can help children whose neurology was affected by early life neglect, abuse, medical issues, or chaos. (Read more about neuroplasticity in Chapter 2.) Over time, *Integrative Parenting* strategies, along

Box 1.3. Gray Matter: Old View, New View

In the 1980s and 1990s, the challenging behaviors of children with a history of maltreatment and caregiver changes were greatly misunderstood by many professionals. Recognition of the profound impact of trauma on children's emotional and social well-being was lacking. Children with attachment problems were commonly conceptualized as developing sociopaths without conscience and driven by rage (Magid & McKelvey, 1987). This view heightened parents' fear and anger and decreased their ability to help their children heal through compassion and emotional support. "Holding therapy," in which children were forcibly restrained, was a widely accepted approach and was believed to help them "release" their anger. Most professionals now agree that there is no empirical support for the method, and that it may have been retraumatizing to many children.

Research in neurobiology and trauma has deepened our understanding of the traumatic underpinnings for the symptoms and behaviors of children who have suffered abuse, neglect, or loss. Psychiatrist Bessel van der Kolk and members of the Complex Trauma Taskforce and the National Child Traumatic Stress Network proposed a new diagnosis—developmental trauma disorder (DTD)—to promote a better understanding of the traumatic roots of the behaviors of children who have experienced maltreatment and other significant adverse experiences in their families growing up. The proposed DTD diagnosis identifies the interpersonal trauma as causal to neurological changes, emotional dysregulation, negative beliefs, and problems in functioning at home and school as well as delays in cognitive, emotional, and social development (van der Kolk, 2005).

Understanding the connection between the children's behaviors and earlier adverse experiences leads to more effective and more compassionate treatment. Informed professionals can help children address their traumatic past to increase feelings of safety and self-worth, and they can guide parents in methods that improve attachment security. Together, professionals and parents can effectively help traumatized children heal.

with effective therapeutic interventions, can improve the functioning of your child's brain.

What Is EMDR?

As we noted previously, *EMDR* stands for *eye movement desensitization and reprocessing*. EMDR has been shown to significantly improve symptoms and functioning in children and adults impacted by traumatic or disturbing experiences. The method reduces distress around the memory and changes negative beliefs to helpful, more positive beliefs. As part of the procedure, your child's EMDR therapist may ask your child to follow her fingers from side to side or follow lights on a horizontal light bar. Alternatively, the EMDR therapist may tap back and forth on your child's knees or hands, or place small buzzers, called *tactile pulsars*, in his hands. The stimulation lights up centers in your child's right and left hemispheres that are vital for processing traumatic material. Through EMDR, stored, unprocessed traumatic memories are linked to adaptive information. The exact mechanisms by which EMDR works are still under debate, but numerous studies have demonstrated EMDR to be an effective trauma treatment.

The Therapeutic Team: EMDR and Family Therapy

Integrative Team Treatment for attachment trauma in children involves both EMDR and family therapy, often provided by two therapists. You will be involved in both the family therapy and the EMDR therapy with your child. The family therapist will help you with parenting strategies and will facilitate "detective work" to uncover the thoughts and emotions driving your child's behaviors. He or she will communicate every discovery to the EMDR therapist, which will guide the trauma work. The family therapist will also help your child develop skills for self-calming and for interpersonal relating.

The EMDR therapist will begin by using the bilateral stimulation to strengthen your child's positive experiences of closeness with you in the therapy sessions. You will be invited to talk about things that will help your child feel loved while he receives the bilateral stimulation; for example, positive early memories, positive traits you enjoy about your child, and things you enjoy doing with your child.

Eventually, your child's therapist will provide EMDR to reduce your child's upset feelings related to current situations that trigger his reactivity. EMDR, as he works through thoughts or memories related to early trauma, will help remove strong emotions and shift his upset thoughts to more positive, helpful thoughts. During this work, as your child is processing thoughts and feelings, you will be asked to be a silent, but supportive, presence. Occasionally, the therapist will invite you to give some input to help your child through stuck places.

By working together with the EMDR and family therapists, your child can be assisted in overcoming stuck thoughts and feelings; in expanding his window of tolerance; increasing his sense of security, safety, and belonging; and calming his reactivity. Over time, your child's brain will develop healthy new connections between his emotional brain and his thinking brain, allowing him to examine his own thoughts and feelings, calm down, and make new choices.

How You Can Promote a Positive Outcome

You can enhance the success of your child's therapy through the following steps:

1. Stay "emotionally present" during your child's therapy. Plan to attend twice a week for perhaps 6–12 months (one EMDR and one family therapy session) followed by a gradual reduction in frequency. At least one parent should be present at all sessions. Each parent should participate at least some of the time.
2. Utilize a support system and find healthy ways to take good care of yourself. Be aware that there will be ups and downs through treatment. Eat right, exercise, and get proper sleep.
3. Take care of your friendships and marriage or partnership if you have one. Find child care and schedule outings.
4. Be open to the methods in this book. Let go of old, emotion-driven parenting practices. In time, this investment of your energy will have an enormous payoff for your family.

IT'S YOUR TURN . . .

Find a notebook and start journaling regarding the following six items. This exercise will help you become more attuned and insightful regarding the feelings and beliefs driving your child's behaviors.

1. List your child's most concerning behaviors.
2. List the traumatic events in your child's earlier life, large and small.

3. Consider your child's current behaviors and early life events. Make a list of possible negative beliefs and survival rules that you guess may be driving his or her behaviors.

4. Make a list of signs that your child is outside of his or her window of tolerance. Divide your child's symptoms into signs of hyperarousal versus signs of hypoarousal.

5. Write down those situations, or triggers, that seem to precede your child's over-the-top reactions.

6. List helpful, positive beliefs you want your child to adopt over time.

Chapter 2

Creating Connections

By the conclusion of this chapter, you will be able to . . .

1. Identify how mindful awareness can help you overcome your emotion-driven responses in order to calm and heal your child's brain.
2. Increase your child's experience of emotional and physical connection with you to begin the process of calming his or her brain.
3. Create pleasurable experiences of connection with your child through play.

MINDFUL CONNECTIONS

It is a busy world these days, and people are finding all kinds of new ways to connect and stay connected with others. Facebook, Twitter, blogging, emailing, texting, Skype, and phone calls connect people worldwide. It is fascinating that any one of us can hop on the Internet and talk to someone halfway around the world in a matter of seconds. Although it is easy to "tweet" or to "talk" with someone on Facebook, some might argue that personal connection is being lost through technology because these interactions are still somewhat anonymous. Others cannot see your face or read your body language (unless you're using Skype). They cannot hear the tone of your voice, and these interactions do not include physical closeness.

We are hardwired to connect with each other, emotionally and physically. *Mindfulness* is a term that describes a state of awareness of our own thoughts and feelings as well as the thoughts and feelings of others. Mindful awareness allows us to communicate and listen and feel connected. Your child desperately needs to feel connected and close in order to heal. He wants closeness with you, but he is desperately afraid of being vulnerable, and so he pushes you away. When his "trauma brain" fires and he moves into hyperarousal or hypoarousal, his behaviors can cause you to feel angry, frustrated, and rejected. You may wonder, "How can I ever develop a close relationship with a child who keeps pushing me away?"

To develop a trusting relationship with a child who is angry and rejecting, you will need to respond in a way that is counterintuitive. Although it feels natural to respond to an angry, defiant child with indignation and disapproval, patience and empathy are the only paths to helping your child heal. Taking these paths will require you to look quietly behind his mask of anger so that you can see the underlying feelings of fear, anxiety, and sadness. To maintain your presence of mind, you will need to stay aware of the automatic emotions that are churning inside of you, while at the same time, you take a step back from the situation and say to yourself:

"My child's behavior actually has nothing to do with me."

Developing the skill of mindfulness will help you avoid becoming part of the problem and allow you to become an agent for change.

WHAT EXACTLY IS *INTEGRATIVE PARENTING?*

After reading Chapter 1, we hope that you have a better understanding of the need for special methods of parenting for children who have a traumatic past. You may have already observed that angry responses to your child's behaviors interrupt those behaviors temporarily but are ineffective in the long run. Understanding the impact of trauma on your child's neurology and belief system, combined with the right tools and delivery methods, will help strengthen his attachment relationships and create the neurological integration and healing your child needs.

Siegel and Bryson (2011) advise parents to help integrate the neurology of their children and develop healthier functioning by helping them develop their capacity to reason and manage their emotions. We chose the term *Integrative Parenting* because a history of attachment trauma frequently leaves children challenged by a poorly integrated brain, and this guide provides skills and strategies that improve neurological functioning. You will learn to use the ingredients of attachment described in Chapter 1—including affection, emotional attunement, and play—to bridge the chasm that separates you from your child. Your developing mindfulness and your application of strategies to calm your child's brain, along with the family therapy and EMDR, will all work together to help your child learn to reflect upon her own thoughts, feelings, and choices, so that she can make effective decisions throughout her life.

MINDFULNESS: CALMING YOUR OWN "SURVIVAL BRAIN"

Simply defining *mindfulness* is easy, but truly understanding and achieving it requires practice and support. Simply put, mindfulness is the concept of being self-aware. Siegel (2010) states that "mindfulness is a form of mental activity that trains the mind to become aware of awareness itself and to pay attention to one's own intention" (p. 86). You may be thinking, "That is way too difficult. I have enough to pay attention to. I am not going to sit cross-legged on the floor and meditate. I don't have the time, and how would that really help my child learn how to behave?"

Mindfulness is a tool that that you can develop over time, even in the midst of a hectic lifestyle. In fact, it can assist you in calming your own brain so that you can better manage your hectic lifestyle and respond to your child in a way that helps him heal. Parents in today's society are pulled in many different directions. There is energy spent working, perhaps juggling a relationship with a partner, and then handling day-to-day challenges with children. As a parent raising a child with a history of attachment trauma, you are faced with the additional struggles of managing the behavioral challenges of a child operating out of survival brain. You have experienced trauma, at least to some extent, during the day-to-day events with your traumatized child, and you may also be operating out of survival brain. You may feel there is no more room in your brain and no more patience left inside of you. Mindfulness can help you . . .

- Become aware of your inner state and increase your tolerance for upset feelings.
- Think things through and take action from a more thoughtful place.
- Let go of self-blame and shame.

Think about how helpful it might be to "just notice" your inner state rather than reacting to all that is going on inside your mind and body.

Finding Calm in the Middle of Chaos

As you have been reading about mindfulness, were you thinking about 100 other things? Were you interrupted from reading this to redirect a screaming child or resolve an argument? Life gets so busy and complicated; you might achieve a calm, mindful state one moment and lose it in the next breath. Remember that you are practicing mindfulness each time you simply take a minute to notice what is going on inside of you.

Building the practice of mindfulness into your daily life will help you learn to be aware of your inner state, without automatically reacting from an emotional place. Mindfulness practice will help you gradually widen your window of tolerance for stress and remain calm with others around you, including your child. Your child's "firing" brain needs your brain to remain mindful and tolerant of his strong emotions as well as your own. Mindfulness and tolerance are twin keys to helping your child heal.

Make a decision right now to develop an intentional daily habit of spending some time with your own thoughts in a nonjudgmental way. Slow yourself down and "just notice" . . .

> Find a point when you have a few minutes of uninterrupted time and sit comfortably or just lie down. For example, sit in the car for a few extra minutes before you unload the groceries. As you sit, notice your breath. Follow your breath for a minute or two as you inhale and exhale. When a thought enters your mind, just notice it, without judgment, and then send that thought on its way. Know that you don't have to act on it or make any decisions about the thought. Gently bring your attention back to your breath. Notice any emotions that surface. Don't judge your emotions . . . just notice them. Know that feelings come and go. Feelings are not right or wrong—they just *are*. We all have them. You don't have to act on your feelings or make any decision related to your feelings at this time. You may notice sensations inside your body. Just notice them, and then gently bring your attention back to your breath. Continue paying attention to your breath as you naturally breathe in and out.

What happened? Were you able to slow down? Did your mind clear a bit? Did you feel calmer and more in touch with your inner state? Or was your mind jumping from thought to thought? If so, that's OK too. Remember, mindfulness means self-awareness without judgments.

You may be wondering, "How will I ever be able to calm my reactive brain, so that I can calm my child's brain? How can I avoid emotion-driven parenting when I get so emotional?" Remember, it takes time to train your brain to observe yourself and ride out your feelings without reacting automatically.

Problem-Focused Coping

Psychoanalyst Peter Fonagy and his colleagues (1997) explain that children develop the ability to notice and think about what they are experiencing only through a loving attachment relationship. When a baby cries and the mother "attunes" and responds lovingly to meet the baby's needs, the baby learns what was making him upset at the same time that he learns what is making him feel better. For example, when a father reaches down to help a toddler back to his feet after falling and gives him a hug, the toddler becomes aware that he was sad and that now he is not. Your child may not have had a parent who attuned and responded in a way that said, "Here is what you are feeling, and here is what will make you feel better." Your child may have had no opportunity to develop mindful awareness of his own inner state.

Another way to describe mindfulness is as *problem-focused coping*. A child or adult who regularly uses problem-focused coping is able to tolerate her emotions so that she can step back and think about them. When we can introspect in this way, we can think about what caused the feeling and then consider our options:

> "Why am I having these feelings? Is there something I should fix? Is there something I need to accept or let go?"

A child or adult who cannot step back and examine her feelings will simply act on them. "Feel it, do it, don't think" might be the motto. "If I feel like screaming, I need to scream." Or "If I feel like running, I must run." Imagine what a difference it would make for your child if you could help her learn to think about her feelings.

If I am engaged in *maladaptive coping* . . .

1. I feel it.
2. I can't think about it.
3. I'll do anything to get rid of this feeling.

However, if I am engaged in *problem-focused coping* . . .

1. I feel it.
2. I think about the feeling, and I think about what is causing it.
3. I solve the problem if I can, or I ride out the feelings until they pass.

If your child lives in survival brain mode, he is wired to "get rid" of his emotions as soon as they surface by either "acting out" or "going away" mentally. He does not know how to stop and think about his feelings. He has a very narrow window of tolerance for his emotions and becomes hyperaroused or perhaps hypoaroused within seconds of having an intense feeling. Your child's therapists will be helping your child learn to think about his feelings, express them, and manage them. Your child will learn to "belly breathe" and to "talk to his brain" with reassuring words to calm himself. The therapists will help your child learn to recognize his feelings and remember that "feelings come and go like ocean waves that wash up over us and then go away."

You will be able to support the therapeutic process at home by developing your own mindfulness so that you can stay calm and attuned to your child's strong emotions. Remember that you and your child's therapists cannot change your child's brain overnight. It will take time to help your child calm his brain and develop the critical process of reflecting upon his emotions and thinking before acting. In the meantime, stay aware of your own inner state . . . and *breathe*.

NEURONS: "I THINK MY CHILD IS MISSING SOME"

Neurons are the core cells within the brain and spinal cord. Neurons possess and send out information, from one neuron to the next, through electrical and chemical signals. Branched projections from the neurons, called *dendrites*, conduct the electrical stimulation by releasing neurotransmitters through chemical *synapses*, which are small spaces between the neurons. Children who have experienced attachment trauma have fewer neural connections in the prefrontal cortex and therefore experience less communication or integration between the various regions of the brain.

The good news, however, is that thanks to the brain's *neuroplasticity*, these deficits can be remedied. One of the most magnificent capacities of the human brain is its malleability. The brain is always changing. Siegel (2010) explains: "Neuroplasticity is a term used to describe the capacity to create new neural connections and grow new neurons in response to experience" (p. 5). In other words, *positive experiences create positive new connections in your child's brain*. When you remain mindful and calm, over time, you are helping your child experience self-regulation and problem-focused coping. Each time self-regulation is achieved, your child actually grows new neurons, which enrich the web of neurological connections between the emotional and logical regions of her brain. Just as an infant develops neural connections by harmonizing with her mother's brain, your child will develop new neural connections for greater brain integration through harmonizing with your mindful, calm brain. Over time, her stronger, more integrated brain will become capable of self-reflecting and problem-focused coping on her own.

Text Box 2.1 explains how specialized brain cells called *mirror neurons* actually shift and change to mirror the brain cells of individuals we are observing (Rizzolatti & Sinigaglia, 2008). As you remain mindful and calm with your child, over time, your child's mirror neurons will shift to replicate your calm behavior. Over time, your mindfulness will give your child the ability to be mindful, which means that he will be able to think and self-reflect before taking action. Imagine what a difference this could make in your child's life.

Box 2.1. Gray Matter: Mirror Neurons

People respond to everyday situations based on previous information that has been hardwired in the brain. Daniel Siegel (2010) explains that specialized brain cells that can mirror the behavior in the brain of another individual are the root of empathy in humans. When we see emotions on the face of another, our mirror neurons shift and move in response, allowing us to literally "feel" what the other feels. Mirror neurons help us understand why children's reactions and behaviors come to resemble the reactions and behaviors of the people who raise them. When children's neurons mirror the calm, predictable behaviors of caregivers, the children experience calm feelings, and those feelings and behavioral patterns become neurologically hardwired. When children's neurons mirror the behavioral patterns of adults who are chaotic, confused, or aggressive, they experience similar chaotic emotions and patterns that become hardwired. Children's behavioral patterns are an automatic response to a hardwired neural network that has been activated. The path to calming dysregulated children is through the creation of new neural networks. When parents respond to reactive, scared children with attunement, mindfulness, and calm, over time, children's emotions and behaviors will mirror the parents' and embed a new network of circuitry in their brains.

INTEGRATIVE STRATEGIES FOR CALMING YOUR CHILD'S BRAIN

Children with a history of attachment trauma can go from 0 to 100 behavioral miles per hour in a split second. Your child is chronically on "high alert": from racing thoughts in her head all the way down to her constantly fidgeting feet. When triggered by a question or a request, you may still find yourself taken by surprise at the immediacy and strength of your child's reactions as she flips into hyperarousal and loses touch with her logical brain. Remember that punishments will not help calm your child's automatic reactions. The goal is to help your child think about her feelings, and over time, to learn to talk about them. Remember, too, that you cannot help your child all alone. Your child's treatment team will also be working on calming your child's brain by increasing her ability to observe her own feelings and thoughts and express herself.

Practice Makes Perfect (or Close Enough)

The best time to help your child learn to calm his brain is when he is already calm. As you connect with him at bedtime and you notice that he is finally relaxed and calm, you can suggest that he notice what it feels like in his body and his brain to have calm thoughts and a calm body. By helping him become conscious and mindful of this calm state, you will help him remember the feeling so that he can return to it. For example:

Mom: Do you want me to rub your back a little after I tuck you in?

Scott [age 6]: Yes, and can you tell me a little story?

Mom: *(Tells Scott a little story while she rubs his back.)* You look all cozy and relaxed. Don't you just love your cozy, warm bed? You are all relaxed, your body is relaxed, your brain is relaxed and calm . . . it's like you are just floating on a beautiful cloud, with nowhere you have to go, just sailing along, easily . . . it feels so cozy, relaxing, easy. . . .

When your child is feeling connected to you and feels safe enough to talk about her meltdowns, you might ask her what she thinks would help her when she starts getting upset. Ask her where she thinks she should go: Is it best for her to go into her room to calm down? Or is she better off sitting next to you and taking some deep breaths with you? Who should go with her, and what does she want you to say to her to help her before she loses control of herself? Keep in mind that once your child goes into a full-blown meltdown, she no longer has access to her thinking brain. Chapter 3 describes the best way to manage the three phases of a major meltdown that has passed the "point of no return." Here is an example of a father and his 11-year-old daughter working together to make a plan for dealing with meltdowns.

Dad: Cindy, that meltdown was no fun for either you or me this morning. Can we figure out some things that might help the meltdowns go away?

Cindy: *(Feels ashamed and puts her head under her pillow.)*

Dad: I know it's hard to talk about, but I just want to help. I was thinking maybe we could figure out a safe, calm place where you could go to help you calm down. We could put some special things in your calm place to help you.

Cindy: How about my bedroom?

Dad: Sure, that would be fine. What do you think could help you calm down while you are in your room?

Cindy: Maybe I could have a punching bag.

Dad: No, I think punching would make you get more worked up. Let's think of something that would calm your brain, instead.

Cindy: I think it might calm me to lie down on my bed with all my stuffed animals and my blanket.

Dad: That's a good idea. Do you want Mom or me to go in there with you?

Cindy: No, but could you stay in the hallway?

Dad: OK, we can try that.

Notice that Cindy's dad discouraged the use of a punching bag. Encouraging physical expression of anger actually intensifies the anger. Many children and parents believe that children need to release their anger through physical aggression. But in reality, "getting the anger out" only escalates the anger and makes it easier to get physical the next time. Using strategies that help your child develop mindful awareness, put her words into feelings, and feel securely connected, loved, and supported will be most effective for calming your child's survival brain over time.

Calming Your Child's Brain through Emotional Attunement

Emotional attunement is one of the four ingredients of secure attachment between parents and their babies. Emotional attunement helps integrate the child's brain. Hughes (2006) explains that emotional attunement increases the child's sense of connection to the parent and calms the child's brain.

Everyone, young and old, wants to be heard and understood. When someone listens to us, acknowledges and understands us, we immediately feel good about the other person. Your child is overwhelmed by many different feelings but has no capacity to express herself verbally. Her emotions manifest as challenging behaviors. To attune to your child emotionally, you may have to make some guesses about the emotions that might be driving her actions. By attuning to your child's feelings, you will help her become self-aware and she will feel connected with you in that moment. When she feels heard and understood, she will be more likely to open up in a conversation with you. By attuning to the emotions beneath her actions and words, you will help your child become mindful of her own inner state.

If your child acts out her emotions in some way, make a tentative statement about what she might be feeling. Don't tell your child what she feels as if you could read her mind. Use tentative wording such as

"I wonder if you are feeling . . ."
"If I were you, I might feel . . ."
"It is normal to feel . . ."

It is a big mistake to tell your child that you know what she is feeling better than she does, why she should not feel what she is feeling, or what she should feel instead. Again, reassure your child that you understand her feelings and that those feelings are normal. Then connect with your child through an expression of affection.

What Not to Do

Five-year-old Theresa is attempting to learn how to tie her shoes. She becomes frustrated, hurls the shoe across the room, and runs into her bedroom, slamming the door behind her. In this example, Theresa's Dad has an emotion-driven response to Theresa's feelings of frustration. The interaction does nothing to help Theresa learn to manage her inner state.

Dad: Hey, there is no reason to slam this door or get angry. It's just a shoe, for heaven's sake. Forget about it!

Theresa: I hate myself! I hate everybody.

Dad: You just stay in this room until you are finished acting up. And from now on, you are wearing Velcro!

Theresa: *(Wails and starts into a major meltdown.)*

In this example, Dad let his own emotions drive his responses when he . . .

1. Lectured
2. Invalidated Theresa's feelings
3. Punished her

He triggered a bigger meltdown, driven by his own powerful emotions, and missed an opportunity to strengthen his connection with his daughter and help her become mindful of her emotions.

Attunement in Action

When Theresa hurls the shoe across the room and runs into her bedroom, slamming the door, Dad continues cooking dinner, giving Theresa time to cool off in her room. Later, Dad knocks and sticks his head in the door.

Dad: Hi, sweetie, I love you. Are you having a hard time?

Theresa: I hate myself! I hate everybody!

Dad: You sound really upset. I wonder if you are feeling frustrated. You know, Steven used to get really frustrated when he first tried to tie his shoes. I understand.

Theresa: Really? Did Steven have a hard time with his shoes, too?

Dad: Oh, yes, a really hard time. Do you want to sit together a bit before we eat dinner?

Theresa comes over to her dad and grabs his hand. She feels connected, which is already calming her brain.

If your child expresses herself to you verbally, restate what your child has told you so that she knows you heard her. Psychologist Ross Greene (2010) recommends that restating your child's thought using her exact language helps her feel assured that you have truly listened and understood what she had to say.

Children need to feel safe and understood in order to open up and express their emotions. Reassure your child that you love him, that he is not bad for having feelings, and that all his feelings are normal.

What Not to Do

Mom: Hi, Steve, how was your day?

Steve [age 12]**:** Crappy . . . I hate school. Mr. Smith is a jerk!

Mom: I don't like that kind of language. You had better straighten up your attitude right now, young man.

Steve rushes off to his bedroom and slams the door. He comes out only when his mom insists he come to dinner, but he remains angry and sullen. By focusing on correcting his language and his "attitude," Steve's mom missed the opportunity to connect with him and to help him talk about his feelings and activate his logical brain in thinking together about possible solutions.

Attunement in Action

Steve [age 12] gets off the bus and enters the kitchen after school. He slams the door.

Mom: Hi, Steve, how was your day?

Steve: Crappy . . . I hate school. Mr. Smith is a jerk.

Mom knows that Steve has trouble in school paying attention and getting work done. It has been a battle since Steve was adopted in second grade. Over the years, Mom and Dad have both worked with the school system to help them understand Steve's strong reactivity to triggers due to his history. It is still an issue even this year, in the eighth grade.

Mom: So you had a crappy day.

Steve: Yeah, I did. Mr. Smith is a jerk—he wouldn't let me turn in my math homework that I finally got finished. He said it would go in the grade book as a 0. You should have never made me do it, Mom, it was a total waste of time. I'm never going back to that class.

Mom: So I hear you saying that Mr. Smith wouldn't accept your old math assignments. I'm sure that really upset you.

Steve: Yes it did, and I am never doing math again!

Mom: I can tell that you are really upset. I understand. I would be upset, too. Let's get a snack and talk some more.

Steve's mom does not address the issue of returning to class and she doesn't focus on Steve's math grade. She simply attunes to Steve's emotions. Attunement helps Steve feel connected to his mom, and the connection calms and regulates Steve's brain. Once he is calm, he and his mom will have a better chance of working on this problem together.

Calming Your Child's Brain by Connecting at Key Times

Emotional dysregulation and feelings of disconnection go hand in hand. Children who feel all alone in the world feel unsafe and anxious. When children feel connected to a parent, even if it is for just a short while, they feel more centered and grounded. The connection to the parent is like a rope that tethers a hot air balloon to the ground. If the rope is untied, the balloon sails off into the air, going who-knows-where. The emotions of the child who feels disconnected will go anywhere and everywhere, with no logical brain to slow them down.

Connection with your child is one of the most helpful practices you can do at home. Touch and emotional attunement are the first two ingredients of secure attachment, and they are crucial parts of the *Integrative Parenting* approach. When practiced together, touch and emotional attunement act like magic on the child's brain. When you notice that your child is "revving up," reach out and give him a hug. When you notice he is getting irritable, encourage him to sit by you for a bit and remind him that you love him. Following separations, even for a few hours, your child is sensitive to how you greet him when you come back together, and this is an important window of opportunity for strengthening his sense of security and trust. Just a few moments of time are all it takes to "tether" your child and help him become regulated in a way that wards off problem behaviors.

Bryan Post (2012) suggests that parents should intentionally connect with their children at three critical points in the day—morning, after school, and bedtime—for 10, 20, and then 10 minutes, respectively. Early morning is often difficult for many children, especially for those who are traumatized. They do not sleep as well, and if they take medication for attentional problems, the medication is not yet in their system upon awakening. In the morning, gently touch your child, rubbing her arm, back, or leg. Talk softly to her as she transitions from a sleep state to a more awake state, easing into the day.

Spend 20 minutes connecting when you reunite with your child after school or work; this helps both of you transition between work/school and home. Instead of firing off questions about your child's day, engage in small talk that remains positive. This is not a time to worry about the night's activities and homework. It is a time to reconnect from the separation of the day and a time to transition into evening activities. This is a tough time of day for your child. She has worked hard and built up stress throughout the school day and may be faced with an evening full of homework or other structured activities that she may or may not enjoy. Remember that your goal is to calm and regulate your child's brain so that she can engage in the higher-level thinking that is necessary for homework. If parents create an after-school atmosphere that is filled with stress, the evening can turn into a battle.

At the very end of the day, spend 10 relaxing minutes with your child, rubbing her back or arms, talking quietly, or saying nothing. These actions help her calm, fall asleep, and stay asleep.

You may be thinking, "Are you kidding me? I don't have 10 minutes in the morning. We barely make it out the door now. Twenty minutes when I get home? Who is going to fix dinner?" Consider adjusting the time to fit your schedule. If 10–20–10 is unrealistic, 5–10–5 might be doable. The method is helpful and worthwhile no matter how long or short it is implemented.

There are many types of behavioral plans that can be used to modify children's behaviors through rewards and consequences. What is most important is how modification techniques are implemented in your home. Any program will be more effective if you can carry out the method calmly, with emotional attunement. By the same token, any program will be ineffective if you are dysregulated—reactive, angry, or fearful.

Helping Your Child with Grief

Most children who are no longer with their biological parents struggle with an underlying grief that becomes acute periodically. Children who do not live with their birth parents may have also lost grandparents, pets, toys, classmates, and other important pieces of their early life. In children, grief commonly leads to meltdowns and self-soothing behaviors such as stealing, hoarding, overeating, and masturbating. Attuning to your child's grief and providing emotional support, understanding, and physical affection will help your child get "unstuck" and perhaps cry or talk, allowing him to move through his grief. He will find comfort and gradual acceptance through his connection with you.

Elisabeth Kübler-Ross and David Kessler (2005), experts on death and grief, identify five stages of grief: (1) denial, (2) anger, (3) bargaining, (4) depression, and finally, (4) acceptance. However, none of us moves through the stages of grief in a linear fashion, completing one stage and then neatly moving to the next. We all move back and forth, back and forth, between the various stages. We can even reach a place of acceptance, and then suddenly be thrown back into anger or depression because of an anniversary date or some other reminder. The good news is that, over time, especially if we are encouraged to share our feelings with someone who is supportive and close, those feelings of anger and despair get smaller and smaller, and periods of acceptance become longer and longer.

When you recognize that your child may be feeling sad about her losses, pull her close. Snuggle your toddler on your lap and rock her, because rocking adds additional comfort and helps bring about emotional release. Invite your older child to sit close on the couch. With an adolescent who resists physical closeness, reach out and lightly touch her hand or shoulder. We have found the best words to say are, "I'm so sorry." Tell her again and again. And tell her, "I'm here for you. Your feelings are all normal, and you will be OK." Over time, you will be surprised at the difference it makes in your child's ability to open up her heart to you.

Martha Attunes to Janie's Grief

Martha described how connecting and attuning helped her work through a period of acute grief with her 3-year-old niece, Janie, whose mother was incarcerated:

> "I had taken Janie to the park, and she was being a terrible pill. Here we were, at the swings and the slides, her favorite place, and suddenly she started hitting me for no reason and shouting, 'You're stupid.' At first I lost my temper a little bit. I raised my voice and said, 'Janie, knock it off. I came here to make you happy. We'll just go home if that's what you want.' I picked her up and carried her, screaming and kicking, to the car. I was really frustrated, and I looked back to see if everyone was staring at us, and then it hit me. All the other kids were there playing with their moms, while Janie was there with her old auntie. I knew then that Janie was feeling grief about her mom, like you had pointed out. So I remembered what you told me about holding her and telling her I'm sorry and all that. I sat down on a bench and started just rocking with her, side to side, over and over. I put my cheek next to hers, and I just kept saying, 'I'm so sorry, Janie. I'm so sorry about your mommy. I'm so sorry. I love you, it's OK. All your feelings are OK. It's OK to be sad, I will help you.'

"Then Janie just burst into tears, and she cried and cried and hung onto me. It just broke my heart. But after about a half hour, she settled down, and do you know? We went back to the slides, and she played and had fun. I am just so thankful you taught me about this, because otherwise I might have just gone and punished her, and all those feelings would have stayed stuck inside of her causing more and more problems. I know this will happen again and again, but I will know now what to do."

Children who have experienced traumatic loss are frightened of the intensity of their own feelings. In family therapy, your child will learn to verbalize his sad feelings, and he will also work through his grief with the EMDR therapist. However, grief itself is not a feeling that moves from a high intensity to no feelings at all. Grief is a process that happens over time and moves from "overwhelming" to "manageable." The therapy will remove the obstacles to your child's grief so that he can process the grief normally, over time. Your ongoing attunement and physical and emotional connection will be a vital component for providing comfort and moving your child toward greater acceptance.

Many foster or adoptive parents have feelings of anger toward their child's birth parents, sometimes due to choices the birth parents made. Remember not to let your own personal feelings get in the way of attuning to the grief and loss experienced by your child. Children grieve the loss of their birth parents no matter how they were treated in the birth home, or when their placement was changed. Negative experiences or complete lack of memory, in the case of a child adopted in infancy, will not prevent your child from experiencing loss and sadness for what "could have been" as well as more complicated feelings of rejection, hurt, abandonment, and confusion. By expressing your anger or disapproval regarding the actions of your child's birth parents, you will add to your child's confusion and may leave her with the impression that her grief is unacceptable to you and must be kept secret. The best course is to set your own feelings aside and discuss them with someone other than your child, so that you can attune to your child's feelings and show empathy.

The Parent's Role in the EMDR Therapy

In preparation for the EMDR work, your child's family therapist will help you and your child build a more trusting connection as well as assisting your child to become aware of, and tolerate, his deep-seated feelings of sadness, grief, and anxiety. Your child must be able to open up his heart and allow himself to experience his vulnerable feelings in order to work through traumatic memories and intense emotions with EMDR. Children cannot be forced to open up if they do not feel safe and prepared. If EMDR is initiated when your child is still afraid of his own emotions, or if he still feels afraid of closeness with you, he will quickly become overwhelmed, and his subconscious mind will shut down his emotions for self-protection. Though you will be a quiet presence during EMDR, your empathy, support, and attunement will help your child feel safe enough and secure enough in his relationship with you to allow himself to think, remember, and feel what he needs to feel to heal.

THE "SERIOUS" ISSUE OF PLAY

Play is fun, but it is more than that. Play and a playful attitude can help you develop an emotional connection with your child through shared pleasure, laughter, and touch. Play is also an important component of your child's cognitive, emotional, and social development. If your child lacked play with attachment figures in her early life, this deprivation may have delayed her development in many areas. If your child missed out on early play, she may now struggle with how to play, and her play may not look like the play of other children her age.

Play helps children learn about, express, and work through their own emotions and the emotions of others. Children even use play to conquer their fears. Play is an important component of developing skills in cooperation and friendship. As they play, children learn to talk, listen, and read others' facial expressions and gestures. Over time, children learn that if they want their friends to play with them, they must share, negotiate, play fair, and be patient.

Play helps children develop imagination and problem-solving skills, while contributing to the development of both gross and fine motor coordination. Watch a group of children "play house." They negotiate who is going to be the mom, the dad, the child, and the dog. They engage their imaginations as they act out their "story." They solve problems as they find props and make a pretend house. Through their "characters" they act out their fears, joke and laugh, and resolve conflicts. In a nutshell, play prepares children to meet the challenges of the adult world, gives them social skills and confidence, and helps them develop the ability to have fun and enjoy life.

Developmental Stages of Play

It is important to understand normal child development and progressions through the typical stages of play. Without those insights, it will be difficult to recognize the developmental differences in your child and understand when progress is occurring. Mildred Parten (1932), a noted University of Minnesota sociologist, identified the developmental stages of play. In the first stage, called the "onlooker," infants of 7 or 8 months of age observe others at play. For instance, the infant will move his head to watch an older child move back and forth on a swing. Though mesmerized, the infant will not reach out or attempt to join the other child. He is content to remain a spectator.

During the second stage of play, "solitary play," the very young child plays with a toy and pays little or no attention to others. At this stage, the very young child will take others' toys without awareness that she is upsetting her peers. This stage often involves repeating actions over and over; for instance, filling a bucket full of blocks, then dumping them out, again and again and again.

Toddlers around age 2 engage in "parallel play," the third stage of play. Two or more toddlers will sit next to each other, playing and talking aloud, without talking about the same topic. In this case, several children may be doing the same or similar things, but without actually playing together.

During the next stage of play, "associative play," children in their early preschool years begin to interact and share. They demonstrate interest in what their peers are doing, but usually have their own theme going during the play. For example, two children may be playing house, but without truly interacting. One may be focused on taking care of the babies, while the other is focused on pretending to make food.

"Cooperative play" is typical in children just starting kindergarten. It is the final and most complex stage, in which children actually play together. They usually share the same theme and interact within the same story. For example, several children may be playing "veterinarian" in an imagined story in which one acts as the vet and the others act as the owners bringing in animals that are sick.

Helping Your Child Catch Up on Play

The absence of normal early play experiences may have impacted the course of your child's emotional and social development. If your child was deprived of opportunities to play, he may be stuck in an earlier stage of play development. Observe your child's play to identify where he is at along this trajectory of play development. The absence of opportunities to play may be related to his inability to express himself, connect cause and effect, and solve problems. Children who have not learned how to experience pleasure through play and friendships are at risk for turning to unhealthy ways to feel pleasure as teenagers. Drugs, alcohol, and sexual activities become the only method available for "feeling good."

Encourage your child's play to progress developmentally by initiating play together and by providing plenty of "true" toys. True toys, such as blocks, dolls, art supplies, board games, and dress-up clothes, facilitate imagination, creativity, and relationship. Moderate your child's use of television viewing and game systems, as they do not facilitate creativity or create closeness. Furthermore, children with attentional problems tend to focus excessively on television and video games and become irritable after playing on game systems for an extended period of time.

Lack of time can also be an obstacle to "true play." Families tend to be over-scheduled in today's world of sports, lessons, and other structured after-school activities. Try to avoid involving your child in too many activities so that she has plenty of unstructured time in which to relax, play, and just "be a kid."

Enhancing Attachment Security through Play

Remember that one of the ingredients of a secure attachment is shared pleasure, play, and fun. Engaging in play with your young child stimulates the pleasure centers in her brain and helps her experience pleasure, closeness, and a sense of security with you. Being playful with your child enhances a happy, trusting relationship with you. Read Text Box 2.2 to learn how play and laughter can change your child's brain chemistry and increase her sense of well-being and connection with you.

If you missed out on infancy with your child, you missed the many opportunities infancy provides for tickling, making faces, and laughing together. During infancy, the baby's mirroring neurons "sync up" with the parent's neurons, organizing the baby's brain and wiring her for happiness in relationships.

It is never too late to begin being playful and having fun with your child to help make up for what you and your child missed in his early life. Find ways to initiate play with your child, no matter what her age. You will help rewire her brain for relationships and create new feelings of connection between you.

Box 2.2. Gray Matter: The Science of Laughter

We all know that we feel really wonderful after we've had a good laugh. Years ago, famous journalist and professor Norman Cousins (1979) discovered that humor and laughter help relieve pain and sickness. The key to the benefits of laughter lies in the chemistry of the limbic region: the emotional center of the brain.

The amygdala and hippocampus, within the limbic region, are involved in detecting threat and flooding the brain with stress hormones, to activate the body for "fight" or "flight" to ensure survival. When stress hormones are released repeatedly, they remain at a chronically high level. As a result, children who have lived for a span of time in a stressful environment continue to perch on the edge of fight or flight.

The limbic area of the brain, including the amygdala and hippocampus, is activated during laughter. Fun, play, and laughter actually increase opioids and reduce the level of stress hormones, leading to overall feelings of well-being and expanding the window of tolerance. Laughter is like a shut-off button to the fight or flight response (Berk et al., 1989). When laughter is shared between parent and child, the positive brain chemistry creates feelings of love and connection between them. Laughter is an important built-in human behavior that regulates the brain and increases health, happiness, and connection.

TIPS FOR ENHANCING YOUR RELATIONSHIP THROUGH PLAY

Due to the effects of trauma on social and emotional development, there may be challenges to incorporating play with your child. The following suggestions will help you avoid some common pitfalls and enhance the pleasure and benefits for both of you.

Tip 1: Stay Attuned by Staying Present

If you are playing together with your child, turn off your cell phone, computer, and take the food off the stove. Your child needs your full attention and presence. When your cell phone dings and you begin texting, your child senses your disconnection.

Tip 2: Stay Attuned by Letting Your Child Take the Lead

By providing plenty of appropriate choices, allow your child to choose and set up the structure of the activity and follow his lead during the play. Your child's play gives you a window into his world. Show interest by "noticing" what he is doing. Don't overly praise; be specific about what you like the most. Here's an example, in which George (age 8) asked his mom if they could color together:

Mom: What are you going to color, George?

George: I'm going to make a superhero.

Mom: I think I will make a dog. I'll take that brown crayon. So what kind of powers does your superhero have?

George: He can turn into rubber and bounce really high.

Mom: Wow, I've never heard of a superhero who could do that. I like the way you are showing how he bounces by drawing those little curvy lines there. That's really creative! I would never think of that.

Tip 3: Be Aware That Your Child's Play Activities May Not Match His or Her Chronological Age

Because children with attachment trauma are often behind developmentally, your 12-year-old boy, for example, may want to play with a train set designed for a 6-year-old. He also might look more like a 6-year-old in the way he plays. He may have difficulty sharing, he may have a need to win, and he may ram trains and trucks together to make big noises. Your 14-year-old daughter might play with dolls meant for younger girls. If you meet your daughter at her level and play without judging, you will connect with her and help her catch up with peers. She might have special dolls that no one else may touch. She might want to play "house" or "school." Do not force her to engage in play activities for which she is probably not ready. Some children naturally avoid engaging in immature play in front of peers, but other children are unaware of social ramifications.

Susan's mother was afraid that Susan, who is 11 years old, would be teased by her peers at day care, so she spoke with Susan about the issue with sensitivity. The following vignette demonstrates her way of communicating with her daughter.

Mom: Susan, can I talk to you about something?

Susan: Sure.

Mom: This summer you will be at the day care when I go back to work. I know how much you love playing with the toys that your younger sister plays with. I have let you take some of her toys that she doesn't care for anymore into your bedroom, and I think that it's just fine for you to play with them. You and I have even played together with those toys, right?

Susan: Yeah.

Mom: But I'm afraid that sometimes kids your age might make fun of other kids who play with those types of toys—even if maybe they secretly want to play with them too. So let's talk about how you can play at the day care without attracting any teasing from the other kids.

Susan: They have lots of art supplies, maybe I could just paint and draw—and make things with clay.

Mom: I think that's a great idea.

Tip 4: Keep It Fun by Finding Ways to Play That You Both Enjoy

You are not a professional actor, and you cannot convincingly pretend to enjoy an activity that you despise. By talking together to figure out an activity that you both find pleasurable, your child will gain practice in the skill of negotiating agreements. Relax, forget about the house or the yard work—it will wait. Laugh, joke, and keep it light.

Tip 5: Playtime Is Not Teaching Time

Don't quiz your child on math problems or colors. Don't ask him to name things or spell things as you play. When you are playing, just play. Comment on what he is doing, stay interested and attuned, joke, smile, and laugh. If you turn playtime into a "lesson," you move away from shared pleasure and fun, and it becomes a task.

Tip 6: If You Observe Your Child Reenacting Traumatic Experiences in Play, Communicate with Your Therapeutic Team

Many children reenact trauma in their play. Trauma play is the brain's way of attempting to gain mastery over terrifying memories. However, trauma play tends to get "stuck," and so the child repetitively repeats the same traumatic event in some form or other over and over again, without healthy resolution. Your child's therapists can help your child move through the experience and integrate the "stuck" memory through therapy.

John is a 9-year-old boy who was removed from his birth parents' home at the age of 2. John wants to play with toys that seem more appropriate for a 2-year-old boy. He doesn't seem to know how to share or take turns, and he tends to engage in "parallel play," avoiding play interactions with his brothers or sisters. John's brain has a natural need to make up for what was missed before, and so he is drawn to the kind of play he didn't get to do when he was 2.

John's parents provided ample time for him to play in order to help him continue down the developmental trajectory in the safety of his forever home. They allowed him to play with toys of his choosing, which included many toys meant for younger children. His parents helped John feel closer to them by setting aside their newspaper and putting off the chores to join John in his play. They found some activities they all enjoyed, including building with blocks and trying on silly hats from the costume box. They used the time to joke and be silly, which made John laugh. As he grew older, John learned to engage in more games and activities with his peers, and by the time he reached adolescence, the gap had closed and he developed some positive friendships.

IT'S YOUR TURN . . .

1. In your notebook, jot down the emotions you experience during stressful times with your child. Don't judge your emotions. Make a commitment to practice staying mindful and increase your tolerance through regular meditation, prayer, or some other healthy method of self-calming.

2. Make a list of times when your child typically seems to be highly sensitive and reactive, such as mornings, dinnertime, homework time, or bath time. Make a plan to purposefully connect with your child at these times through emotional attunement and touch.

3. Take a moment to reflect on your family's weekly schedule. Analyze how much unstructured time you and your family have to relax and have fun. Ask yourself, when was the last time I played with my child? Set aside some intentional time to relax and have fun with your child. Each time you do, you will be helping your child heal and strengthening your relationship. If you have a younger child, bring out the art supplies, board games, or a ball. If you have a preteen or teenager, make a commitment to take time to just "hang out" together each week, or start a daily ritual of playing a game of cards or sharing a snack together.

Chapter 3

Solutions to Challenging Behaviors

By the conclusion of this chapter you will be able to . . .

1. Identify situations that directly trigger your child's behaviors.
2. Identify situations that leave your child more vulnerable to acting out or melting down.
3. Identify negative thoughts and feelings ("dominoes") that may be associated with your child's behaviors.
4. Identify the attuned *Integrative Parenting* responses you would like to implement in response to your child's most concerning behaviors.

Parents often come to therapy with a list of behaviors that are troublesome and interfering in their daily life situations. Some behaviors exhibited by traumatized children can be scary, dangerous, exhausting, and seemingly never-ending.

This chapter outlines specific methods that, in conjunction with therapy, will help heal and integrate your child's reactive brain so that over time, he can learn to think about his feelings, calm himself, and make effective choices. *Integrative Parenting* is not focused on teaching your child lessons or finding punishments that will motivate him to behave. *Integrative Parenting*, influenced by the work of Siegel and Bryson (2011), is designed to calm your child's brain, help him become aware of his own emotions and thoughts, and integrate his logical thinking brain with his emotional brain. In order to carry out the *Integrative Parenting* strategies effectively, it will be important for you to continue practicing mindfulness so that you can stay in a calm state.

"SCARY" CHILDREN, "SCARY" PARENTS

Children with a history of severe trauma can sometimes look and sound "scary." Meltdowns that last for hours, name-calling, screaming, and sometimes property damage can occur. Frightened parents often don't know what to do or even how to attempt to get the child under control. Parents have power when they understand the emotions beneath the behaviors. "Scared" children have "scary" behaviors. Traumatized children are scared of being vulnerable and scared of rejection and abandonment. Because they experienced the world as a threatening and scary place, they believe "I'm not safe and I have to do what I can to protect myself."

When your child begins to have a big, scary moment, you probably think, "Oh, no, here we go again." You become scared of what will happen next, and so *you* act scary. The more extreme your response, the more dysregulated your child becomes. Scared children act scary, parents become scared, and then they act scary, and around and around they go. Figure 3.1 illustrates this scary cycle.

Now imagine this scenario. Your child starts to act scary, but you are regulated and calm and using attunement skills. Your neurons are calm and you are mirroring that calm to your child so that she can move back into a state of calm. This is how the cycle of "scary" is broken. Your child needs your calm, regulated brain to

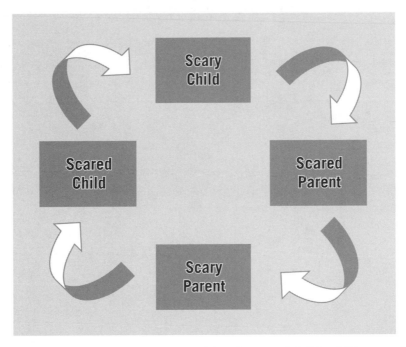

FIGURE 3.1. The "cycle of scared" illustrates how the scared child exhibits scary behaviors, leading to scared parents who look scary, too. Scary parents, in turn, heighten the child's fear.

help her feel less scared, which will stop the scary behavior. Figure 3.2 illustrates this calm cycle.

RATIONAL THINKING FOR PARENTS

Let's think back to Chapter 1 and the information you learned about the neurological impact of trauma on your child's beliefs. Following is a list of rational ideas that can help you avoid emotion-driven reactions to your child's difficult behaviors:

• "My child wants to be close, but he is sure that he will be rejected."
• "My child is terrified of being vulnerable."

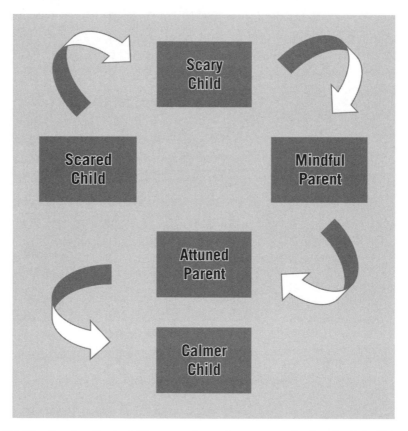

FIGURE 3.2. The "cycle of calm" illustrates how the parent who is mindful of his or her own internal state can stay calm and attune to the feelings driving the child's behaviors. The end result is a calmer child.

- "My child needs to feel in control in order to feel safe."
- "My child has a hole inside he needs to fill in some way."
- "My child had to find some ways to soothe himself."
- "Wants feel like needs to my child."
- "Trauma changed my child's brain."
- "My child's behaviors are reflexive and automatic and stem from his survival brain."
- "My child does not know how to fix his own neurology."
- "When my child is hyperaroused or hypoaroused, he cannot think or behave rationally."
- "My child is not evil or bad, he just lives in his survival brain."
- "With the right tools, I can begin the process of healing, calming, and integrating my child's brain."
- "I can make an enormous difference in my child's life with the right information and strategies."

TWO TYPES OF MELTDOWN

Meltdowns are no fun—they are no fun for parents, siblings, or other family members and definitely no fun for the child experiencing meltdowns. Siegel and Bryson (2011) describe two types of meltdowns: "downstairs" and "upstairs." The downstairs meltdown is driven by the lower regions of the brain—a brain that is "firing" due to some type of trigger. The "upstairs" meltdown, more commonly called a tantrum, is an entirely different phenomenon. Children choose the upstairs (upper cortex) meltdown consciously—in an attempt to force their parents to give them something.

Upstairs and downstairs meltdowns are considered typical behaviors in children 5 and younger. Almost every parent has experienced the embarrassment of a screaming toddler in the candy aisle of the grocery store. However, young children with a history of attachment trauma may have multiple tantrums per day and downstairs meltdowns that last for hours. It is not uncommon for traumatized children to exhibit meltdowns at elementary school-age or into adolescence. Some traumatized children are very prone to the upstairs tantrum due to a core negative belief, "I have to be in charge of getting what I need"—and everything they want feels like a need. Sometimes upstairs tantrums develop because in the child's very early life, her parents were unable to tolerate any crying, and so her cries were rewarded with sweets or other bribes. Sometimes the "chosen" tantrum gets the adrenaline and cortisol flooding the brain, and the child ends up in complete hyperarousal, which leads to an out-of-control, downstairs panic meltdown. If your child begins a conscious tantrum for a prize, but ends up in a downstairs meltdown, you still have to manage it as a downstairs meltdown. Later, when everything is calm, you can attune to the "wanting feeling" that started the whole thing. Your child's therapists will also work with your child on her meltdown triggers. They will help your child understand the difference between *wants* and *needs*.

You may be wondering, "How can I tell if my child is experiencing an upstairs tantrum to get his prize, or experiencing a downstairs meltdown, in which his brain has lost control?" There are several clues. First, if your child is choosing to tantrum, he can stop on a dime if something catches his interest—with no aftereffects. Secondly, when he becomes certain that he is not going to achieve his prize, he will stop and move on with no aftereffects. The work in therapy will help both you and your child begin to understand the differences between the 2 types of meltdowns.

It is imperative not to reward a tantrum with things or candy, and it is especially important to be absolutely resolute when the tantrum escalates. If your child is choosing to tantrum to achieve a prize, you might say:

> "This is not something you need, this is something you want—I love you, but the answer is no."

Do not negotiate, plead, or bribe. Deep breathe, use earplugs, or imagine a scene from your favorite movie.

It is important to stay mindful of your own feelings as your child begins a conscious tantrum driven by "wanting." Emotion-driven parent behaviors such as yelling, lecturing, or spanking can be perceived as rejection or abandonment, turning an upstairs tantrum into a full-fledged downstairs meltdown. If you are at home, stay calm, stay nearby, and fold laundry, do dishes, or make the meatloaf. If you are at the grocery store and she is small enough, pick her up, leave your cart in the aisle, inform the checker, and leave the store. If you have an older child, you may need assistance from a store clerk. The clerk could assist with the purchased items, and you can assist your child in getting to the car. Modulate your voice, and keep your eyebrows slightly elevated, not furrowed.

Our colleague, Ann Potter (2011a), has developed a way of understanding the progression of a typical downstairs meltdown along with management strategies that parents are finding extremely helpful. The theory identifies three specific phases of a meltdown:

- Phase 1: Acting out (panic)
- Phase 2: Acting in (shame)
- Phase 3: Repair and reconnection (emotional pain)

Each phase has distinct characteristics and specific parent management tools. Meltdowns can be reviewed and dissected in therapy. Your therapist can help you identify the different phases and coach you on how to handle your child specifically. Let's take a closer look at a meltdown in order to gain better understanding of the different phases.

Flora came into a family therapy session and described her grandaughter's meltdown as follows:

"My 8-year-old granddaughter, Leah, had come home from school in an angry mood. Every attempt to interact with her had been met with an angry retort of some sort, and I found myself growing increasingly weary and frustrated. Through dinner she continued to be grumpy, whiny, and difficult. My husband and I invited her to sit between us and watch a children's show after dinner, but the behaviors continued.

"I decided that she was just overtired and needed sleep. I invited her to put on her pajamas for bed, and then the giant meltdown started. Objects in her bedroom began flying through the air, and her body turned into what looked like a flopping fish on the bed. My granddaughter was pulling all the bedclothes off the bed as she was rolling around and screaming, 'Go away! Get out of here! I don't want you here!' My instinct was to get angry, but because I understand more than I ever did before about meltdowns, I took a deep breath, sat down on the floor, and said, 'Wow, I wish I understood what you are feeling.' I stayed very quiet while she rolled and shouted for a little while longer, and then she suddenly reached out for me as she began sobbing uncontrollably. I got up next to her and took her in my arms and held her. I rocked her side to side on the bed as she continued to sob. My heart broke for her when she cried, 'It's not fair! All the other kids live with a mom and dad. Their parents are married, and they are young, and they have a house and brothers and sisters and they do fun stuff as a family. My parents were never even married. I hate going to my dad's house; I don't even like all those kids over there, and I feel uncomfortable. I don't even get to see my mom that often. I don't have brothers or sisters here to play with, and I just feel so, so sad.'

"I continued to hold her and rock her and I said, 'I'm so glad you could tell me,' and I said, 'I'm so sorry,' over and over, until she calmed down, like you've taught me to do in the family therapy sessions. Then my husband came in, and we took turns holding her and telling her how much we love her. She gave us big hugs and told us she loved us, and then settled right down and went to sleep. The evening could have ended in anger, but because I was able to attune to all that grief and sadness beneath her big meltdown, it became an opportunity to help her with her grief and make her feel more secure with us."

PHASE 1: ACTING OUT—PANIC

Phase 1 of a meltdown is a child's version of a panic attack. Imagine that something has triggered your child and no parenting strategy has worked, and so a meltdown has begun. At this stage, your child's brain is stuck. The emotional limbic area of the brain has been activated and the prefrontal thinking part of the brain is not operational. Your child is in a state in which he cannot tell the difference between present and past, and he may be experiencing an emotional flashback—that is, a recurrence of intense emotion associated with a past trauma. He has no conscious insight into his overwhelming feelings. His survival brain is activated and he is in flight or fight. He is verbally and/or physically out of control, and in this stage, touch is typically not tolerated. This stage can last anywhere from a couple of minutes to several hours.

In the example above, Leah was clearly having a difficult time upon her arrival from school. Flora attempted to help Leah calm herself, but nothing seemed to be working. Flora fed her and tried to help Leah relax, but to no avail. They were headed into Phase 1 of the meltdown, no matter what. Phase 1, in this example, is identified by the complete loss of control of Leah's emotions and actions. Her prefrontal cortex had shut down, and there was really no way that Flora could have "talked" or "threatened" Leah out of the Phase 1.

Managing Phase 1

Handling Phase 1 requires some very specific strategies. In this phase, your child requires some physical space around her. You may be able to invite her to her room or another part of the house, where she can safely have some physical space, while you stay nearby. Attempting to close in on her, however, will likely activate a stronger fight response, and she may react like a cornered animal. Once the child is in a full-blown meltdown, telling her to calm down or threatening her with punishment is not helpful and may trigger greater emotion. Her logical brain is not online.

Throughout Phase 1 of the meltdown, let your child know that you are still present and that you care about her. Try to keep yourself as calm as possible. Because they are caught up in intense emotions without access to the rational, thinking region of the brain, children are not fully present in the body during this stage. This is called dissociation. Your calm voice and presence can help ground your child and may shorten the length of the meltdown.

If you have a partner, make a plan to tag-team in this situation, so that one stays nearby while the other takes a break. This will help you manage your own energy level and keep calm. Give yourself reassuring messages such as . . .

"I can handle this."
"Her survival brain is firing, but it will burn itself out soon."
"She is not in her logical brain."

Once Flora decided that Leah was in Phase 1, she sat close, calmed her own voice, and just attuned to Leah. Flora did not try to stop Leah from throwing things or screaming. If she had, the meltdown would have escalated. Flora also stayed close but gave Leah space at the same time. Leah was screaming "Get out of here!" but she didn't really mean it. Flora gave her enough space without leaving. With older children, if they ask you to leave the room, standing just outside the door (without appearing to be blocking them in) can be a reasonable distance.

You may be able to help prevent a meltdown by reassuring the dysregulated child, using connecting strategies, and calming her brain with your own calm brain. But you will not be able to prevent every meltdown. Again, once the meltdown has started, the child is incapable of stopping it any more than an adult can stop a panic attack once it has taken hold. At this stage, it is best to just let her move through the meltdown. Your job is to make sure that she is physically safe, reassuring her that you are there, no matter what.

PHASE 2: ACTING IN—SHAME

In Phase 2, your child's brain is still stuck; the prefrontal cortex is not engaged. At this stage, your child may be embarrassed by what has just happened, and he is flooded by shame. His negative beliefs about himself are activated, such as, "I'm a bad kid" or "No one loves me" or "No one can handle me." Although he does not express these thoughts explicitly, remember that they are present and continue to trigger the very overwhelming emotions that he is feeling. The child in Phase 2 is beginning to come back into his body, back to the present, and he may be sobbing in despair, or he may be withdrawn inside of himself. If you move closer, he may continue to push you away, yelling, "Leave me alone!" or "Don't ever talk to me again!" or "I hate you!" In the next breath, he may yell, "Don't go . . . don't leave me." You may feel pushed and pulled. He doesn't want to think that he needs you, because it feels too vulnerable, but he *does* need you at the same time. The fear of rejection or abandonment is strongly activated, and he experiences an emotional flashback to earlier situations in his life in which he was rejected or overwhelmed by shame.

It is very difficult to discern when a child has left Phase 1 and is in Phase 2. It may gradually become clearer as you begin to deal with meltdowns using this method and you notice different signs and signals that your child uses as he enters and then moves out of each phase. Your therapist will help you dissect your child's meltdowns, and you will all gain insight into what happens in the different stages that are specific to him.

Leah moved to Phase 2 once she started to talk and explain why she was so upset. Flora let Leah say what she needed to say. Flora did not interrupt or try to correct Leah's thoughts or beliefs. If she had, Leah probably would have moved back into Phase 1.

Managing Phase 2

Managing Phase 2 is very similar to managing Phase 1. Continue to provide the appropriate amount of space, but as your child moves through the phases, you will probably be able to move the boundary closer. If he is in his room, you may be able to sit on the bed instead of standing in the hallway.

Nurturing messages of love and safety are necessary. The primary feeling during this stage of the meltdown is shame. Now that he is becoming more grounded in the present, he may feel embarrassed and shameful that he lost control. He may think that he is going to be in big trouble for having this meltdown.

You should continue to help reorient your child to the present moment. Ground him with questions such as, "Can you feel your feet on the ground?" or "We are in your room—can you notice the color of the walls?" Once you sense that your child is grounded, it is not necessary to continue asking those types of questions. At this stage, there is very little real conversation going between you and your child. His logical thinking brain is still not fully operational. At this point, he may be able to tolerate some touch, but perhaps not. Attune and respond to what he needs.

In the meltdown example between Leah and her grandmother, once Leah allowed Flora to hold her, Flora knew that Leah was present and thinking again. Grandma did a wonderful job of listening and attuning to Leah's sad feelings about being different from other kids and missing her birth mother.

PHASE 3: REPAIR AND RECONNECTION—EMOTIONAL PAIN

Once you cross into Phase 3, you know that your child's brain is finally unstuck. The prefrontal cortex is engaged again, and she is fully back in the present. In this stage, she may be feeling intense shame about what has just occurred, and she is likely terrified that you will reject or abandon her. She feels overwhelmingly alone in the world.

In Leah's meltdown, the hugs and expression of love composed the repair work done after this meltdown. Grandma and Grandpa did not lecture or scold Leah for having a fit, screaming, and throwing stuff around. There was no need to punish any of Leah's behaviors. Leah may have been triggered by something said at school or even a thought or memory, and she could not manage it. Her grandparents did a wonderful job of managing this meltdown. Over time, they hope that Leah will learn to express her feelings and thoughts without being so overwhelmed by them.

Managing Phase 3

During Phase 3, it is time to draw your child close and reassure him that you are glad he is back and is feeling better. Touch is important in this stage. He needs to connect with you physically and emotionally in order to fully repair the relationship. There can be some quiet, gentle talking at this stage, but this is still not the time to discuss what happened, what he can do the next time, and what he will need to fix (if something was broken). This conversation, if it is necessary, can occur later in the day or even wait for the family therapy session. If this discussion occurs too soon, while the child is still feeling some anxiety and shame, it could trigger another meltdown.

Meltdowns are exhausting and at times scary. If you learn to manage them in a mindful, attuned way, and implement strategies to strengthen the attachment relationship and heal your child's past, the meltdowns will gradually wind down. Over time, your child will become more regulated and able to manage his triggers, thus preventing the loss of complete control.

Managing a Meltdown in Action

Suzie spent 2 years in foster care when her mother was struggling to recover from a drug addiction. Now fully in recovery, Suzie's mother is learning strategies to improve the connection and calm Suzie's brain, but Suzie still has occasional meltdowns. On this occasion, Suzie had spent the night with a friend and had come home exhausted, so her brain was taxed. She asked her mother for a popsicle, and her mother replied, "I'm fixing lunch right now, and you can have a popsicle for dessert." Suzie's brain, in her exhausted state, could not manage the "waiting feeling," and she fell into Phase 1 of a meltdown. Suzie fell on the floor and began writhing and kicking, while wailing loudly. Suzie's mom reminded herself, "This is Suzie's trauma brain. She is getting better, but she is overtired. I can handle this."

Mom: I'm giving you some space, Suzie, but I'm right here. As soon as your brain calms down, we'll snuggle and talk.

Suzie: (Continues meltdown at full throttle on the kitchen floor for about 10 minutes, while her mom waits quietly off to the side.)

Mom: Remember, Suzie, you are here in the kitchen, and I am here nearby. I love you. When you are calm, we will snuggle and talk.

Suzie: (Curls into a fetal position;, begins sobbing). [Beginning Phase 2 of the meltdown]

Mom: I'm still here, Suzie. I'm coming into the kitchen, OK? I love you.

Suzie: Go away! *(Continues to sob.)* No, don't leave! *(Calms down and reaches for her mother.)*

Mom: *(Moves in and holds her, rocking her back and forth.)* I love you, I'm glad you are calm. How about we eat lunch and then have a popsicle together?

THE DOMINOES

Many tiny steps lead up to a meltdown and other difficult behaviors. If parents become more mindful of the small steps and use *Integrative Parenting* strategies, many meltdowns and other acting-out behaviors may be prevented. Ann Potter (2011b) has termed the chain of events leading up to the meltdown as the *domino effect*. Do you remember setting up a string of dominoes as a child and then watching them rapidly fall, one after the other? In situations with your child, a string of dominoes can fall almost as rapidly. In family therapy, your child's therapist will help you and your child "put on your detective hats" and identify the dominoes leading to meltdowns and other behaviors. This is done in a matter-of-fact, nonjudgmental manner meant to reduce feelings of shame and embarrassment. Increased awareness of the most common dominoes that lead to your child's meltdowns will help you find opportunities to change their direction and, over time, will give your child the power to make new choices.

Vulnerabilities

Your child will be more vulnerable to big behaviors when he is already somewhat dysregulated due to other situations. These are just a few of the situations that might leave your child on edge and unable to tolerate negative thoughts and feelings when they are triggered:

- Recent lack of sleep
- Hunger
- Not feeling well physically
- Mom or Dad on edge due to his or her own mood problems, conflict, or job stress
- Recent punishments for misbehavior
- School-related stress
- Grief triggered by some recent reminder of the biological parents

Andy celebrated his 11th birthday on Saturday. His parents were amazed that he managed his behavior throughout the entire day. He kept himself relatively calm, he used good manners, he ate a reasonable amount of cake, and he thanked everyone for his gifts. On Sunday morning Andy woke up very crabby and was headed toward a meltdown by noon because his brother ate a piece of his cake without asking. Andy was vulnerable to a meltdown because he was mentally exhausted after putting forth so much effort the day before to keep himself in check through all the excitement and activity. Instead of taking away his new presents because he got mad about the piece of cake, Andy's dad took some time to sit with and connect with him. Andy's dad validated how hard Andy had worked to keep himself under control the day before, and how tired he must feel. He validated Andy's sad feelings about the cake and helped him get back on track by becoming mindful of his tired feelings.

Triggers

Think about situations that trigger negative emotions and thoughts for your child. They may be situations that trigger fears of being unsafe, hungry, alone, rejected, or deprived, or feelings of shame, hurt, vulnerability, powerlessness, or anger. Triggers could include:

- Parent's angry face or voice
- Teacher's angry face or voice
- A bad grade or a detention
- Preoccupied parent
- Being asked to do a chore
- Homework time
- Morning
- Bedtime
- Siblings

There are certain triggers that you may be able to help your child avoid, but there are many triggers that are unavoidable. With help, children can learn to become mindful of their own triggers. When your child is calm, bring up the topic of triggers. Explain to your child that triggers are situations that cause us to have sudden big feelings. Share your own triggering situations, including situations that have nothing to do with her. If she is receptive, ask her if she can name her triggers. As both you and your child become more aware of triggers, your child's tolerance and increased capacity to think through things will become stronger, thus helping prevent full meltdowns.

Big Emotions

Big emotions are part of the chain of toppling dominoes. An emotion can be triggered automatically and reflexively by a situation, by thoughts, or by body sensations. An emotion can be a trigger to more emotions, to negative thoughts, or to body sensations, and emotions can definitely lead to big behaviors. Common emotions that are difficult to tolerate without becoming dysregulated include:

• Shame and guilt
• Anxiety
• Anger
• Frustration
• Powerlessness
• Hurt
• Grief

The intensity of your child's emotions can go from 1 to 100 in a split second. Attuning to these big feelings is critical when the dominoes begin falling. Your child needs your emotional attunement to begin understanding and verbalizing his internal state. Noticing your child's emotions and acknowledging them without judgment will help him become more accepting and more comfortable with feelings. He needs your reassuring presence when he is talking about, thinking about, or experiencing feelings to help him know that he can have feelings and still be OK. Remember that when children are experiencing intense emotions, they believe they will never feel any other way, and they don't feel normal or safe. When the timing is right, remind your child that feelings come and feelings go, and that all feelings are normal.

Helping your child develop tolerance for his feelings will require a tremendous amount of practice and emotional support from you and your child's therapeutic team. Remember that the goal is to help your child believe that he can experience her feelings and be OK, and that you are there to help and support him.

Negative Thoughts

The child with a history of attachment trauma has developed many negative beliefs about himself, others, and the world, and his most negative beliefs will come to the forefront when he is triggered. Just a few of the many negative thoughts that may be triggered include:

- "My parent/teacher is mean."
- "I'm not safe."
- "I'm a bad kid."
- "I'm not good enough."
- "I can't do anything right."
- "I don't belong."

Look at the negative beliefs held by your child that you listed after reading Chapter 1. Now read through the positive truths/beliefs that you want your child to hold. At home, however and whenever you can, gently remind your child of positive truths such as, "I'm always here for you" and "You are an important part of this family."

Body Sensations

Body sensations can be part of the chain of toppling dominoes. Children with a history of attachment trauma are often very cut off from their body sensations, yet unconscious awareness of uncomfortable sensations often increases the intensity of their behaviors. Frequently, children interpret the body sensations that accompany their emotions as illness. We can all relate to uncomfortable sensations that accompany intense emotions, including:

- Heavy chest
- Headache
- Tension in neck and back
- Sick feeling in stomach
- Trembling

Body sensations are signals to the brain that something is up. Watch and listen for body sensations to help you attune to your child emotionally. At times they may be hard to detect, but if your child complains of a headache or stomachache, be aware that she may be heading toward dysregulation and a meltdown. Teach your child about how her body talks to her and gives her signs that it may be time to discuss something or ask for help.

Gladys, age 6, is having trouble on the weekends. She becomes very easily angered, and her patience level with her siblings is almost nonexistent. Her mom tries to get her to take a nap or do a quiet activity because she knows that Gladys expends a lot of energy during the school week and is simply worn out by Saturday. The following vignette illustrates how Gladys's mom is helping her become more aware of her body sensations.

Mom: *(Listening to Gladys, who is outside on the swing set, yelling and bossing her siblings around.)* Gladys, can you come in the house for a minute? I want to talk with you.

Gladys: What, Mom? I'm playing—I don't want to come inside. I'm not doing anything wrong. They are not playing the game right.

Mom: I'm sure that is true. Sometimes your brother and sister want to play their way, don't they, and that upsets you. It's hard to be the big sister. I have another question for you, though. I'm wondering if your brain and your body are telling you that you are tired, and the tired feelings are coming out in your words? Do you think that could be true?

Gladys: I'm not tired. They are just being mean.

Mom: Hmmm, I'm wondering if your brain and body worked so hard this week doing all that great schoolwork that they just need to rest a bit. Let's sit down on the couch together for a little while and see if that is what is going on inside. *(Gladys stomps over to the couch and sits down. After a minute, she has a big yawn.)* That was a nice yawn. I wonder if your body says, "Hey Gladys, let me rest. I'm tired."

Gladys: My feet are tired.

Mom: Yes, I bet they are. Maybe we should let them rest here on the couch. What about your brain? Is it tired?

Gladys: I don't know.

Mom: Gladys, it's OK to take a break and rest. I think your body and brain would play so much better with your brother and sister if you just took a rest. I will stay with you on the couch, and we can rest together.

Gladys: *(Falls asleep for about a half an hour and wakes up.)* Mom, you were right, my brain was tired. I think it is rested. Can I go back out and play?

Mom: Yes, you sure can.

If Mom had made Gladys come in and take a nap, a meltdown probably would have occurred. Mom is trying to help Gladys become more in touch with her body so that she can learn to read her own signs.

The Final Domino: The Meltdown or Acting Out Behavior

The meltdown or other acting-out behavior becomes the final domino toppling over. When you begin thinking in terms of dominoes, you will learn to start thinking backwards from the big behaviors to the dominoes that preceded the final crisis. This will give you important information that may help you help your child change course when he is headed for a problem. After a crisis, when both you and your child are calm, you may be able to sit down and calmly examine the dominoes that led up to the "storm" together. This nonjudgmental, logical approach to examining the chain of events activates your child's logical thinking brain, minimizes the shame and emotional reactivity, and encourages problem-solving that may help prevent a problem the next time.

Debriefing a Meltdown

Thirteen-year-old Ted had had a meltdown at dinnertime. He had complained about the spaghetti and his mom had told him he could go to his room if he didn't like it. He had stormed off to his bedroom and stayed there the rest of the evening. Before bed, his mom asked if she could come in so they could talk.

Mom: Was it a hard day at school today?

Ted: I had a headache all day. Algebra is stressing me out. I keep forgetting to bring my book home, and now I'm behind.

Mom: I can understand that must be stressful.

Ted: And I didn't eat lunch. The food was disgusting at school today.

Mom: You must have been really hungry. And then you had to go to football practice after school.

Ted: Yeah, and the coach really worked us, and it was hot.

Mom: That must have been hard.

Ted: My coach yelled at me. I forgot the play. I felt like an idiot.

Mom: I'll bet you were still beating yourself up about football and algebra when you got home.

Ted: Yeah.

Mom: I wish I had known what a hard day you'd had. I'm sorry I reacted so strongly to the spaghetti comment. It just hurt my feelings, and I had a stressful day, too. From now on, let's both try to communicate better when you come home, OK?

Ted: OK.

Mom: Why don't you come to the kitchen and get yourself something to eat.

Ted: OK. And then do you think you could help me figure out this algebra assignment?

Mom: Sure.

Preventing a Meltdown

Erika, age 10, has a developmental delay in addition to a history of attachment trauma. Dad notices that Erika seems agitated as the family is preparing to leave for church on Wednesday evening. Last Wednesday evening, they didn't make it to church because Erika had a full-blown meltdown.

Dad: Come here, Erika. Let's snuggle on the couch for a few minutes. I love you. Tell me how you are doing.

Erika: I don't know. I'm kind of mad.

Dad: How come? What are you feeling?

Erika: Nobody pays attention to me. Everybody is busy. My friend Mary says she isn't my friend anymore.

Dad: Wednesday evenings are busy, aren't they? I can understand that you feel like you don't get enough time with me or with Mom, and I had no idea you were having problems with your friend at school. Tell me more about it. . . .

By spending some time connecting and attuning to her feelings, Dad is calming and integrating Erika's brain and warding off the pending meltdown.

UNDERSTANDING OTHER COMMON "SCARY" BEHAVIORS

Children with a history of attachment trauma feel insecure and unable to turn to parents for comfort or help. This is a miserable way to live in the world. As a result, the children live in "survival brain," as we've mentioned, which means that they will do whatever they think they need to do in order to . . .

• Protect themselves
• Comfort themselves
• Self-regulate

Your child had to learn strategies to self-protect, self-comfort, and self-regulate in her early life. Even though her situation changed, her survival behaviors did not. Remember that her old thoughts and feelings are hardwired into her brain. When triggered, scared feelings and thoughts are activated, triggering earlier strategies for self-protection, self-comfort, and self-regulation by default.

Think about your child's early life. How do you imagine she protected herself? Did she learn to scream and cry to demand the attention or food she needed? Did she learn to shut down and withdraw in order to avoid getting hurt? Did she learn to take food surreptitiously so as not to attract attention? Did she learn to lie to avoid repercussions?

What do you believe she did to comfort herself? Did she learn to self-comfort with sweet or salty things, when there was little comfort available? Did she learn masturbation or sexual touch as a way of getting good feelings?

Even children who were removed from situations of neglect quite early are hardwired to mistrust the adults who care for them, and they continue to fear that they will not get enough of what they need—food, attention, or comfort. It sometimes takes only a few short weeks for the brain to wire itself for survival during infancy.

THE LITTLER HURT CHILD INSIDE

One way to understand how thoughts from your child's early life continue to drive his current actions is through the concept of the "inner child." Deep down, we all have a smaller "child self" within—made up of the youthful hurts, insecurities, and fears that can echo inside of us in our most vulnerable moments. In our therapy sessions, the children we work with intuitively understand this concept. The children become more self-aware as they contemplate, in a given moment, whether or not they are operating from their "big-boy" or "big-girl" self, or whether it is the "smaller child within" who is in charge. We encourage the children to appreciate their smaller child within for coping in whatever way was needed. We model this appreciation by saying, for example:

> "When you were little, you had to be really strong and mad in order to get your needs met. We should thank that littler, mad part of yourself for helping you survive."

Alternatively, we might say:

> "When you were little, you learned not to get close to anyone because people kept leaving. We should be grateful to that littler you inside who tried to protect you from any more hurt by pushing people away."

At the same time, we help children recognize that now it is time for the big-girl or the big-boy self to do things in a different way. Helping children live and deal with issues in their "most grown-up self" is an important component of healing the wounded inner child.

Speaking to the Littler One Inside

Often, we encourage children and their parents to dialogue with the littler child inside. For example, we might say to the child:

> "Let's talk to the littler you inside and reassure him [her] that he [she] can relax and stay safe inside your heart. Let's tell him those difficult events are all over, and that you are safe."

Parents, too, can help heal their child's traumas by giving messages of reassurance to the littler child who lives inside their child's heart.

In a similar way, we encourage children to "talk back" to their feelings, or "talk back" to the emotional part of their brain. Most children have never thought about talking to themselves. The concept of *self-talk* is often new for parents as well. Self-talk is an important tool for self-regulation and for enlisting the logical brain to help manage the emotional brain. Self-talk integrates the emotional and logical regions of the brain and calms the child. Following are some vignettes that illustrate how you can encourage your child to self-talk. Perhaps these scenarios will encourage you to dialogue with yourself in a similar way.

Inner Child Talk in Action

Sandra, age 8, has just gotten out of bed, and like many children with a history of attachment trauma, she has woken in a regressed, angry state.

Sandra: Mom! Come here right now. I need you. I need you right now!

Mom: *(Entering the room)* I didn't hear you get up. *(Attuning and connection)* It sounds like you woke up kind of upset. Come snuggle with me on the bed for a minute.

Sandra: I'm starving. I need breakfast right now! I can't wait!

Mom: *(Gently pulling her into her lap and giving her a hug)* You know, I will never let you go hungry. I want to remind "littler Sandy" who lives inside your heart that everything is OK. I want to tell her that she can trust me to make you a good breakfast this morning. Maybe you can talk to the little Sandy inside, too. Now would you like eggs, oatmeal, or cereal for breakfast?

Sandra: *(Calm now)* Will you fix the eggs like you fixed them yesterday?

Mom: Sure.

Brain Talk in Action

In another example with a 14-year-old boy, Terry, self-talk was a helpful coping skill for dealing with a new experience. Terry was going to attend a 2-day overnight basketball camp away from home. Because of his emotional and social delays, this was the first time he would attend something like this since he was adopted at age 7. Like many children with a history of attachment trauma, he didn't think of talking to his parents about his anxiety, but he was visibly agitated the day prior to leaving for camp.

Dad: Terry, why don't we sit out on the porch for a bit while Mom is fixing dinner? You know it would be very, very normal to feel nervous about going to camp. This is your first camp away, and lots of kids get a little nervous about that. Do you think you might be feeling a little nervous?

Terry: Yeah, maybe.

Dad: Remember how we can use our smart thinking brain up here in the front to talk back to those feelings? I wonder what your smart thinking brain might tell the nervous part of your brain to help calm things down inside?

Terry: Um, everything's OK?

Dad: Sure, you can talk to your brain and say, everything is OK. You might say, "I'll be with my good buddies, Sam and Dave. I met the coaches, and they are really nice. And it's just for 2 days, and it's only a half hour away. If I needed anything important, my parents would be there in a jiffy." Do you think you can tell your brain all that?

Terry: Yeah, OK.

LYING

Lying is one of the behaviors that parents most want their children to stop. Telling the truth is at the core of a trusting, close relationship. All parents deal with lying to some extent. Most children occasionally tell a lie to avoid a punishment or get something they want. However, children who have a trusting, close relationship with their parents want their parents' approval more than they want "stuff," and for the most part, they trust that their parents love them and want the best for them. Usually, a questioning or disapproving look from the child's parent will trigger a truthful confession, and a "little talk" about the importance of trust will make a strong impression with the securely attached child.

For traumatized children who believe that the world is unsafe, lying is crucial for survival. The child operating in survival brain lies reflexively to avoid punishment. Lying may have prevented your child from getting hurt in her early life. Lying has become so automatic to your child that she has trouble recognizing the difference between a lie and the truth.

Some children with a history of attachment trauma also tell a different kind of lie—we call this lie the "tall tale." Do you remember the tall tales of Pecos Bill and Paul Bunyan? Children with a history of attachment trauma often tell huge whoppers for no reason because they lack a strong sense of self. They missed out on those lovely early experiences of learning about "I" and "thou" and feeling both lovable and loved. There is a hole inside and a natural need to fill the hole by inventing a self. These children often carry strong negative beliefs such as "I'm invisible," "I'm alone," and "I'm insignificant." The made-up stories seem "as good as real" and make children feel like they are important. What is true and not true gets all mixed up in their brains. Your child's family therapist will work with your child to develop mindfulness regarding what is true and accurate and what is false, and the EMDR therapist will work on changing the negative beliefs driving your child's impulses to lie.

Responding to the Lie with Mindfulness

In order to stay calm and mindful with your child, remind yourself:

"My child is operating in survival brain. The truth and the lies are all mixed up in his [her] brain."

71

This approach will help you avoid emotional reactions that are ineffective. Responding to the lie in an attuned fashion would sound like this:

> "I know this is hard for you, but we need to work on being accurate with your words."

Over time, your child's reactive survival brain will calm down, and he or she will learn to trust and begin to tell the truth.

Robert was supposed to complete his homework for dinner so that he could go to soccer practice that evening. Robert is 13, and he was adopted 2 years ago. In the following vignette, Robert's mom is helping him learn to be accurate with his words.

Mom: *(At the dinner table)* Robert, were you able to finish all of your homework? I think you had some math and a language arts sheet, and you were supposed to read a chapter in your novel, is that right?

Robert: *(Head down)* Yeah, I'm done. I'm going to get to go to soccer practice, right, Mom?

Mom: Yes, Robert, you will get to go, but sometimes it's hard for you to tell me that you have not really finished your homework. I also thought I heard the television on when you were working on your homework. [Mom is careful with her tone of voice and she uses words that are not accusatory in nature. Her goal is to help Robert learn to tell the truth and to feel more comfortable doing so.]

Robert: I wasn't watching television, Mom. You always think I'm watching television.

Mom: Robert, it's OK. Remember, I love you and want the best for you, right? I know that homework is not your favorite thing—especially reading, right? If you didn't have time to finish all of your work, let's work out a plan so that it gets done and you can go to soccer practice.

Robert: *(After a long pause)* Mom, I didn't read the chapter. It is a stupid book, and I hate it.

Mom: Thanks for telling me, Robert. Did you finish your other assignments?

Robert: Yep, I will show you *(picks up his math and language arts homework)*.

Mom: Great, these look good. Let's read the chapter together when you get home from practice. How does that sound?

Robert: OK.

In this next example, 10-year-old Betty has experienced a series of relative place-ments that didn't work out, and she recently came to live with her Uncle Tom and Aunt Jen. Uncle Tom understands that Betty has a history of telling stories to get attention and that she has very poor self-esteem. He lets Betty know in a kind way that he doesn't believe her tall tale, and he attunes to the emotions driving her storytelling behavior.

Uncle Tom: How was school today, Betty?

Betty: A bunch of kids got hurt on the playground at recess. Some bigger kids from the neighborhood came onto the playground and started throwing rocks and sticks. An ambulance came and took all the kids to the hospital. It was really scary!

Uncle Tom: Betty, it's OK if you had an ordinary day at school. I'm interested in just ordinary things like what you had for lunch and how you did on your spelling test. Let's try this again and be really truthful with your words, OK?

Betty: You don't believe me. I'm telling the truth, Uncle Tom.

Uncle Tom: Honey, I would love to believe you, but I'm having a hard time with it. I still love you, though. Come here and let's take a look at that spelling test.

Betty: *(Hanging her head)* You're not going to like it.

Uncle Tom: OK, you were just scared I was going to be mad about this test, weren't you? *(Betty nods.)* Hey, I had a hard time with spelling as a kid, too. We'll work on this so you can do better on the makeup test.

Try not to ask your child a question that sets him up to tell a lie. If you know he has broken a rule, let him know that you have "observed" him break the rule or that you have clear evidence that he has broken the rule. For instance, let's say that one day your 12-year-old complains that her new pack of gum is missing. You notice a trail of gum wrappers in the living room, and at the end of the trail, you find your 10-year-old sitting on the floor watching television, chewing gum. The set up: "Did you take your sister's gum?" You already know the answer, and you also know that he will reflexively lie and claim he did not take the gum (even while chewing the gum). As a result, you are mad at him for lying *and* taking the gum. Instead, let him know directly that the evidence is clear and that you wish to have a discussion about why that was not OK.

DEFIANCE

Most parents deal with defiance in their children from time to time, especially over things children tend to dislike, such as homework, chores, or curfews. However, the securely attached child who trusts her parents ultimately wants their approval more than she wants to misbehave. Defiance in most children is a temporary situation. For traumatized children, however, defiance is sometimes the norm, whereas cooperation is the anomaly. Your child's defiance is another type of survival response. Your child may have developed a very strong-willed part of herself when she was very young, which allowed her to cope with a situation over which she had no control. Her survival brain tells her that you cannot be trusted and that she has to be in charge of making sure that she gets what she needs and wants. When you do things as a parent to keep her healthy and safe and teach her right behavior, she assumes that you are mean. Your child's therapeutic team will be working with your child to help her change her negative beliefs, trust you to be in charge, and think through her reactions before they build into defiance.

Responding to Defiance with Calm Attunement

To stay calm and attuned, remind yourself, "My child thinks I'm against him. I need to help him know that I'm on *his* side." An attuned response to your child's defiance is this:

> "I love you. It's my job to keep you safe. It's my job to guide you. I'm on your side."

Following is a short vignette between a mother and her 10-year-old son, Anthony. Anthony is an aggressive child who has a hard time letting adults be in charge, especially his mother. The following situation depicts a conversation in which Anthony has refused to take out the trash, which is his weekly chore. The situation is already escalating a bit because whenever Mom approaches Anthony with a question or comment about chores, Anthony becomes very defensive.

Mom: Anthony, I noticed that our trash was not out this morning for pickup.

Anthony: I took the trash out, Mom.

Mom: Anthony, I know how much you dislike chores and sometimes feel like you have to do all the chores around here, but I notice that the trash cans are still sitting by the side of the house. [Notice here how Mom does not get in a power struggle about the lie.]

Anthony: So, they can get the trash next week. Why can't Sarah [younger sister] take out the trash? She never does anything around here.

Mom: Sarah has her chores also. She cleans the bathroom and sweeps the kitchen. Let's not worry about what Sarah does. How are we going to solve our trash problem? I am worried that we will have too much trash by next week.

Anthony: *(Says nothing.)*

Mom: *(Waits patiently)* I think I have an idea. You can go to the Smiths' across the street and ask if we can add our garbage to their garbage. Their side of the block gets their trash picked up tomorrow.

Anthony: Whatever.

Mom: Help me understand what "whatever" means. Does that mean you will go and ask?

Anthony: Yes, OK, Mom.

Mom: Thank you. When you get back, let's sit down together and discuss the chore list so we can make sure things run a little more smoothly.

STEALING

Yes, stealing is against the law, and children who take things from stores, school, or the homes of friends are in fact stealing. But stealing, too, is a survival response. If your child cried and no one responded to his cries with what he needed—whether food, a clean diaper, or touch—he learned to believe, "No one cares—I have to be in charge of getting what I need." Your child learned to think, "I have to take what I can get in the moment, because I may not get it later." His brain can't distinguish the difference between what he wants and what he needs, and he feels like he will die if he doesn't get what he thinks he needs.

Securely attached children sometimes experiment with stealing a bit, as a way of testing the boundaries or showing off to friends. But traumatized children can exhibit very significant stealing behavior. Your child may be stealing very small things on a regular basis or occasionally stealing very valuable items such as technological gadgets or money. Stealing can land a child in trouble with the law, so working on this behavior with your child's therapeutic team is imperative.

Responding to Stealing with Calm Attunement

As triggering as this behavior can be to parents, a mindful, calm approach is still vital in the healing process. In order to remain calm and attuned, remind yourself, "Wants are needs to my child." An attuned response to your child is this:

> "I know it feels to you like this thing will make you happy. I know that it's hard for you to trust that I will give you what you need. But stealing behavior is not going to give you a happy life. This is something we will need to ask the therapist to help us with."

Over time, your child will stop stealing as she learns to trust you, as she feels secure and loved, and as she develops a sense that she is lovable and worthwhile. Following is a short vignette between Elizabeth (age 9) and her mother.

Mom: Elizabeth, I was putting some papers in your backpack for school and I noticed some lip gloss.

Elizabeth: Yeah, I found it.

Mom: *(In a very gentle, soft voice)* Hmmm, I was wondering if the lip gloss came from the mall the other day. Remember, we had stopped at the mall to get you some new shoes, and we stopped at that bath store and you asked me for some lip gloss? I remember saying no. [This gentle approach will keep Elizabeth's brain regulated so she can continue to participate in the conversation and solve the lip gloss issue.]

Elizabeth: Yes, I remember, but I found the lip gloss *(looking down and her voice is escalating)*.

Mom: [Knowing that Elizabeth stole the lip gloss, Mom chooses not to engage in a power struggle over whether or not Elizabeth is telling the truth, which would have gone nowhere, but instead to attune to the emotions driving the behavior.] Elizabeth, I know how much you like lip gloss, and I know that you do not like it when I tell you no. Remember, *no* doesn't mean that you will never get any lip gloss again, and the lip gloss really cannot make you feel better. Later, I have to run an errand. We can return the lip gloss to the store together. We can't take things that are not ours.

Elizabeth: Do we have to?

Mom: Yes Elizabeth, we have to. Taking things that are not ours is not legal. It is against all the rules.

BATHROOM ISSUES

Toilet training can be a challenge, even when a child is in a stable, loving home. Many children in intact homes begin using the toilet regularly and then regress upon starting a new day care or a preschool. Securely attached children who are heavy sleepers can struggle with bed-wetting, sometimes into adolescence. However, early caregiver disruptions and traumatic events can lead to severe bathroom issues that last for years. Children who lived in a chaotic environment or moved from placement to placement before the age of 2 may have missed critical developmental stages when they would have learned about their bodies and toilet training. Furthermore, children operating out of a survival brain lack mindful awareness of the body sensations that tell them they need to go to the bathroom.

The Underlying Causes for Bathroom Issues

Because of their inability to recognize their body sensations, many traumatized children have trouble with wetting the bed at night or wetting their pants or having bowel movements in their pants during the day. Children who lived in chaotic circumstances in early life may not have received adequate assistance with learning about their body sensations during the appropriate developmental window, and so they are not able to notice their body's cues or even smell the wet or soiled pants. Some children were not given adequate milk and liquids as infants and developed constipation and started avoiding having bowel movements because it was painful. Some children have a condition in which the colon has stretched so that now there is no urge to have a bowel movement. Problems with wiping feces on the wall may be related to a lack of bathroom skills and a feeling of panic. Sometimes more severe behaviors such as playing with feces or urinating in strange places are related to a traumatic past and dissociation or emotional regression to an earlier age of functioning. The bathroom itself may be a trauma trigger for some children. And, yes, some traumatized children who cannot verbalize their emotions may go to the bathroom in the corner of a room because they do not know another way to express their angry feelings.

Children with bathroom problems should be examined by a pediatrician to rule out the possibility of any underlying medical concerns. There are medications that help with nighttime wetting, and a bowel softener can help with lack of adequate bowel movements or a stretched colon. An occupational therapist can help with lack of sensitivity to the need to go to the bathroom or to wetness or soiled pants. A physical therapist may be able to help with wetting problems by helping the child to train the muscles that control the bladder. Your child will be working with the family therapist to develop new bathroom habits and skills. The EMDR therapist will reinforce new patterns and work to heal traumas and change any negative beliefs or upset emotions that may be driving his bathroom behaviors.

Most children with enuresis (wetting themselves or the bed) or encopresis (uncontrolled bowel movements) have a great deal of shame. They may have fallen off the typical developmental trajectory due to early traumatic events. Problem patterns have become very entrenched. To effectively help children with bathroom issues, parents need a great deal of patience, mindful thoughts, and actions. If your child has bathroom problems, remind yourself, "My child missed this window of opportunity to learn these skills." Following are examples of attuned responses:

- "Honey, I'm here to help you with this. Let's clean this up together."
- "I think this might be about some big feelings you have been experiencing inside. When we go see the counselor tomorrow, maybe she can help us figure out those feelings and help us find a way to talk about them together."
- "Let me show you how to use the toilet paper and how to flush and wash your hands."
- "Dad is going to show you how to aim into the toilet, and then he'll show you what to do next."
- "Honey, let's go over what the doctor told us. A little of this medicine each day will help make your poo softer, so going poo won't hurt anymore. But also, he said it is very important that you spend some time on the toilet each morning before school to give the poo plenty of time to come out. What can we do to make this easier for you? How about we put some of your favorite puzzle magazines in a basket right next to the toilet."
- "OK, sweetie, let's remember what the doctor said. No drinks before bedtime, and use the bathroom just before bed. But you still might need to go to the bathroom during the night. I know you've been scared about getting up in the night, so I'm leaving the light on in the hall to help. But if you still feel scared, call me and I will help you, OK?"

It will be very difficult for your child to change any long-time patterns that have become entrenched. A simple reward chart can be helpful to provide that extra motivation the child needs to keep the changes in the forefront of his mind.

For example, you might put up a sticker each time your child uses the bathroom appropriately and reward him with a trip to the ice cream parlor together as soon as he has earned his first six stickers. (To make the goal achievable, do not insist that your child earn the stickers sequentially. In other words, if he misuses the bathroom, he does not need to start over.) Continue with the reward system until the new pattern has become automatic for your child.

Following is a vignette between a mother and her 7-year-old daughter, Katie, who has ongoing issues with wetting herself and not wiping after using the bathroom. Not wiping her bottom has caused some skin irritation and some odor problems. Katie is just leaving the bathroom.

Mom: Katie, did you remember to wipe?

Katie: *(Doesn't answer, but runs outside to play.)*

Mom: Come here a second, sweetie. *(Katie comes running. Mom speaks in a quiet voice.)* I just went in to the bathroom and noticed that you had forgotten to flush the potty and that there was no toilet paper in there either. I am wondering about that.

Katie: I did wipe, Mom. I don't know where the toilet paper went.

Mom: Let's do this. Let's have you come back inside for just a minute and we'll make sure you aren't damp. We need to make sure that rash gets better.

Katie: No, I don't want to.

Mom: I know this is hard for you, but it is no big deal. Sometimes it is hard for you to remember to wipe. I will show you one more time, and you can practice. Let's do it together, and you can go right back out and play. [It is hard for Mom to stay patient with Katie regarding this issue, so Mom works very hard to stay mindful of her face and voice tone. She has learned that Katie can't learn when the feeling of shame triggers her.]

Katie: OK, but I hope this doesn't take forever.

Mom: It won't.

AGGRESSION

All children, especially toddlers and preschoolers, occasionally hit or kick, shout, or threaten. Probably few mothers can say their child has never said, "I hate you." However, children with a history of attachment trauma lash out more frequently and with more vehemence than children raised in more optimal circumstances.

Their attachment figures are usually the recipient of their aggression, but siblings, peers, and even teachers may struggle with the child's aggressive behaviors.

Children who had a chaotic early life are wired for "fight" mode. Their meltdowns turn aggressive very quickly. Once their brains start firing, they are not in control, and they may not be fully present. Later, children often do not remember things they did or said. In addition to learning how to manage the three phases of the meltdown, the most effective way to calm your child's aggression over time is through consistent attunement, talking over triggers and feelings, and helping your child feel secure and loved. Over time, feeling connected to you and learning to identify and talk about what she is feeling will be key to calming her reactive brain.

GETTING THE ANGER OUT

Many children have a sense that hitting, kicking and screaming helps them "get the anger out." Once they begin hitting, kicking, or screaming, they quickly leave their window of tolerance and move into hyperarousal, where they no longer have any conscious controls. Some therapists believe that children need to "get the anger out," so they instruct them to beat on a pillow when they are angry. The truth is, hitting, kicking, and screaming—or beating on a pillow—only increases the overall disorganization in the child's brain. Children who are instructed to beat on a pillow will be more likely to have another meltdown the next day. Ask your child if she believes she has to have a meltdown to "get the anger out." Remind your child that that statement really is not true. Remind her that it is harmful to her brain when she has a meltdown because it is like "anger practice" for the brain. You, your child, and the family therapist will help your child develop skills, practice self-calming, and develop a plan to implement at home. The EMDR therapist will be working with your child's angry thoughts and anger triggers. For example:

• *Ed's plan:* Ed told his parents that he needed to be allowed to go to the basement and be alone when he starts to become angry. Ed said that he could get away from the big feelings by lying on the basement floor and going through his card collections.

• *Susan's plan:* Susan and her parents decided to turn her room into a calm space by flanking it with soft blankets, pillows, stuffed animals, favorite magazines, and her CD player with her favorite CDs. Susan found it helpful to bury herself in her animals and blankets and put on her headphones.

Choosing Anger Over More Vulnerable Feelings

Children who lacked early nurturing dread emotions that make them feel vulnerable. Sadness, grief, loss, hurt, and fear are avoided at all costs. One simple way to avoid those vulnerable feelings is to work up a "mad" feeling to push away the "sad" or the "hurt." Notice if your child tends to get mad when his feelings are hurt, when he has suffered a loss, or when he is anxious about an upcoming change. If this is the case, help him understand why mad feelings are not the best choice and reassure him that you can help him with the other feelings.

Following is a vignette between Evan (age 10) and his biological mother. Evan spent 2 years in foster care while his mother was working on her recovery from depression and drug addiction. His mother has noticed that he has episodes of aggression whenever something happens that should cause him to feel sad. Evan's aggression has escalated since his grandmother died a week ago. Evan's mother now attempts to entice Evan to let her help him with his vulnerable feelings instead of acting out aggressively.

Evan: I hate you. Get away from me.

Mom: Evan, I would like to talk with you for a minute.

Evan: No, go away.

Mom: Do you know that I am here for you, no matter what you are feeling? I know that you must be feeling sad about Grandma, and I think you need some more time cuddling and being close to me right now. I want to help you, not fight with you. Will you come snuggle with me? And let's talk about all the fun memories with Grandma.

Evan: *(Moves up onto the couch and lets his mom snuggle with him.)*

Following is a short conversation between 13-year-old Miranda and her adoptive mother. Miranda's reactivity and aggressiveness are related to her mistrust of caregivers. She has a history of early abuse and several changes of foster homes before finding permanency. In this situation, Miranda has asked to go to the mall with her friends, but her mom had to stay no because of a previously scheduled doctor's appointment.

Miranda: Mom, my friends and I are going to the mall this afternoon. Will you drop me off at 2:00?

Mom: So your friends are going to the mall, and they want you to come and be there at 2:00? *(Checks to make sure that she understands what Miranda is asking, because Miranda has the belief that her mom never listens to what she says.)*

Miranda: Yep.

Mom: Miranda, I know how much you love going to the mall with your friends. Today we have an appointment at 3:00, and my concern is that you would get to the mall and then have to leave again almost immediately. It just doesn't look like that will work out today.

Miranda: *(Begins yelling and tossing her clothes around her room, becoming increasingly agitated.)* You never let me do anything! I *am* going to the mall! I will walk! I am not going to the stupid appointment! I hate you!

Mom: I can see how upset you are, and I know how much you like going to the mall with your friends. Let's sit down and talk a minute about how we can solve this problem.

Miranda: I am going to the mall whether you take me or not.

Mom: I can see that you are really upset. I would be happy to work out a solution if we can just sit a minute and talk calmly. I think we can solve our problem.

Miranda: *(Still very agitated; Mom waits quietly.)* What?

Mom: Well, we have had this appointment at 3:00 for several months, and my concern is that we won't be able to get in for another couple of months. Do you think you could contact your friends and talk with them about finding a better time to meet at the mall this weekend?

Miranda: They probably won't be able to go, so no.

Mom: Well, my concern is that we would not be able to change this appointment. We have to get this done before school starts again, but I am not trying to keep you from having fun. I like seeing you have a good time with your friends. This is a good opportunity to practice problem-solving. My suggestion would be to contact your girlfriends about rescheduling, and we will go from there.

Miranda: *(Calms down after a short time and asks to use the phone.)*

Note that when Miranda began screaming and throwing her belongings around the room, Mom chose not to address the behaviors, but instead attuned to the sad and disappointed feelings Miranda was experiencing. Later on, when Miranda was in a calm state, Mom asked her to sit down so they could talk about what had happened. Mom reminded Miranda that the idea of "getting the anger out" with aggression is harmful to her brain, and that calming her brain gives her a healthier brain. Because Miranda had been working on developing self-awareness in therapy, she was able to name her emotions and identify coping skills that could have helped. Miranda agreed to work on taking deep breaths, lying on her bed, and using some self-talk. Later, Miranda was able to talk about the incident in family therapy, and she worked through her identified triggers with EMDR.

FOOD ISSUES

Securely attached children can have food issues related to avoidance of new tastes or textures, an obsession with sweets or junk food, or a tendency to be thin or heavy. Children with a history of attachment trauma have some specific types of food issues that are not as common for children in intact families.

Like bathroom behaviors, serious food issues are often related to deprivation in early life. Sneaking or stealing food from cupboards and hoarding food are two of the most common behaviors that frustrate parents of children who suffered early deprivation. Stockpiles of candy or other goodies may be found under beds, in closets, or in drawers, and parents fear the food will cause a bug infestation or rotting food smells. Another common food issue is gorging on large portions that add extra pounds.

It is important for parents to note that fear of being without food is a hardwired survival response. People naturally have a heightened fear of starvation when they have experienced a span of time without adequate food. When children have known hunger to a point of fear during early life, that fear becomes entrenched. The desire to hoard, stockpile, and gorge is reflexive and natural—and it is one of the most difficult fears to eliminate.

Calm Attunement to the Hardwired Fear

It will be helpful to emotionally attune to your child's fears that there won't be enough and provide reassurance—over and over and over:

> "Sweetie, I know you worry about having enough food, but at our house there is always plenty of food, and we will always make sure that you get all the good, healthy food your body needs."

However, don't expect complete elimination of this fear. Because it is so hard-wired, some anxiety about food may be present forever. Many parents find it helpful for children who hoard to have some healthy, wrapped items in a special snack basket in the bedroom. It can also be helpful to have healthy snack foods on hand in the cupboard or refrigerator.

Remind the anxious child that there are healthy snacks available, or reassure her that her hunger will be satisfied with a meal very soon. For instance, you might say:

> "Honey, remember, we're eating in just a few minutes. You won't have to wait long. What can you do to keep busy and make the time pass?"

When a child carries extra weight due to overeating or gorging, it is vital to avoid shaming or embarrassing the child. The more shame the child experiences around his urges for food, the more overwhelmed, anxious, and out-of-control he naturally feels, increasing his need to self-comfort with food. An attuned and reassuring response will be much more helpful in managing the child's cravings. For example, you might say:

> "Sweetie, let's think together. What do you think would be a healthy portion? I know it might feel like it won't be enough, but remember, you will have a snack in 3 hours, and then a short time after that, you will have dinner."

Think of yourself as your child's emotional coach, not the prison warden guarding over the food.

Food refusal and failure to thrive, strange eating habits, and sensory issues related to food textures or tastes often occur in this population of children. Your child's therapists may want to include an occupational therapist or nutritionist as part of the treatment team. Emotional attunement, nurturing, and connecting with your child through touch, eye contact, and play are crucial for healing her deep-seated food compulsions. Family therapy and EMDR are critical components for helping your child develop new ways of managing her emotions, reducing reactivity to food triggers, changing negative beliefs and emotions related to food and traumatic memories, and developing a stronger sense of secure attachment in her relationship with you.

SEXUALIZED BEHAVIORS

Securely attached children in intact families may exhibit some behaviors that could be described as sexual. It is not uncommon for toddlers and preschoolers to begin exploring their own bodies or "play doctor" with one another out of natural curiosity. Children of any age may discover good feelings related to touching themselves that subsequently turn into a habit for self-soothing. Typically, younger children can be redirected to another type of soothing activity, and older children can be taught about "private parts" and how to behave modestly.

Sometimes, children with a history of attachment trauma have acquired sexualized behaviors that are not easily redirected. Sexualized behaviors can be extremely frightening and triggering for parents. Many children have become wired for excessive masturbation because they spent months or years without the nurturing they needed, and rubbing their own genitals was the only means they had of comforting themselves. When masturbation has become a primary method of self-comfort for a young child, the behavior may be very entrenched. As the child gets older, the focus on his own genitals may expand to exploring the genitals of other children, or even animals.

Some children have witnessed parents behaving sexually or have been exposed to pornography in their earliest environments, or they may have been the victim of some form of sexual molestation or assault. Children's responses to exposure and assault vary widely. Some children are extremely traumatized, and their sexual behaviors are subconscious reenactments of the early events. Trauma reenactment is a phenomenon that has been recognized by experts for many years. Children can be observed acting out their early experiences in their interactions with others or in their play, because their brain is having great difficulty working through the experience. It is like a CD with a scratch, playing the same melodic phrase over and over, unable to move on and complete the entire song. The child may have "stuck" images or feelings that drive sexual behaviors over, and over, and over.

For some children, sexual arousal feelings were experienced as good feelings that provided relief or comfort during early sexual abuse events that were also confusing and scary. The child who experienced early arousal feelings may become fixated on reexperiencing the sexual feelings, and seek the arousal compulsively. No matter how intentional their behavior appears, it is important to remember that they are only children, and their behaviors and compulsions are part of the damage caused by their early abuse.

Safely Addressing Sexualized Behaviors

The best place to address sexual reactivity is with your child's therapeutic team. Your role is to stay mindful and calm, by saying to yourself, "This may have been the only kind of touch he knew," or "He has unhealed trauma stuck in his brain." Respond to your child's behaviors with attunement. For example, you might say, "We will work with the therapist on this. We love you no matter what."

Educating the sexually reactive child regarding body parts, privacy, sexual feelings, and boundaries is crucial. It is essential to educate without shame, as shame is accompanied by fear, self-hate, and anxiety, which send the child into hyper-arousal and the very same coping methods you want her to stop.

Of course, safety is the first priority—safety for the sexually reactive child and safety for other children in the vicinity. If you have a sexually reactive child, you will not be able to send your child off to play with others unsupervised. Your child's family therapist will help you make a plan to ensure safety for everyone. You will need to have very clear rules for your sexually reactive child and the other children in the home. For example:

- "One person at a time in the bathroom."
- "The bedroom is a place to play alone, not with others."
- "We don't hide under a blanket with a playmate or sibling or hide together anywhere."
- "We leave our bedroom dressed appropriately."

The family and EMDR therapy will help your child work through the memories and emotions that subconsciously drive the sexualized behaviors and help your child develop new and healthier ways of comforting himself and interacting with others. Your emotional support will be critical to your child's healing process.

Following is a vignette involving an adoptive mother and her young son, Marcus (age 6). Marcus was the victim of sexual abuse by an uncle when he was very young. Marcus has recently exhibited some sexualized behaviors in relation to his younger sister, who is 4. Marcus's mother has just walked into the family room where Marcus and his sister have been sitting on the couch, watching a movie. Marcus is lying on top of his sister.

Mom: Marcus, please let your sister sit up.

Marcus: *(Shouting)* Leave me alone! I wasn't hurting her—we were playing.

Mom: Everything is OK, Marcus. But the rule is, we sit up on the couch side by side to watch a movie.

Marcus: *(Runs out of the room, knocking things off the end table.)*

Mom: *(Following Marcus to his room)* Marcus, can I come in and talk? You are not in trouble. Sometimes it is hard to remember the right way to play with your sister so that you both have fun and feel safe.

Marcus: *(crying)* I wasn't hurting her.

Mom: I know you weren't hurting her. I know you love her, but your brain has to remember the safe ways to play. How about if we talk about it with Miss Stefanie? We can practice how to play safe with Miss Stefanie.

Marcus: OK.

Marcus's mother set a boundary and then attuned to Marcus, minimizing his shame and moving him back into his window of tolerance. She knew that this was a therapeutic issue, so she made a good decision to save any further discussion for the therapist's office.

CONCERNING WORDS

Children with a history of attachment trauma do not have the ability to express themselves effectively. Your child most likely shouts words to communicate that she is upset, but she does not use words that accurately describe how she feels. It is natural to feel hurt, overwhelmed, or angry when your child hurls angry words at you. Try using the section below to "translate" your child's verbal onslaught to the words that represent what she really means deep down. This will help you remain mindful and calm and respond with attunement to your child's emotional state.

When he/she says . . .
- "I hate you."
- "I wish I was dead."

What he/she really means is . . .
- "I hate the way I'm feeling."
- "I want to escape from these feelings."

- "I'm going to kill you."

- "I wish you had never adopted me."

- "I would be happier with my first parent."

- "You're stupid."

- "I'm hurt and I'm angry with you for my hurt."

- "I feel like I don't belong."

- "I'm grieving the loss of my first parent."

- "I'm upset and I don't know how to talk about it."

A DEEPER UNDERSTANDING

By now, we hope you have a deeper understanding of the traumatic roots to your child's behaviors. Children with attachment and trauma issues do not like thinking the way they think, or acting the way they act. However, they need our help in learning how to cope with their old memories, change their current beliefs, and manage their triggers. You are probably now much more aware of the emotions that drive your own reactions, and you are learning to be more mindful, attuned, and intentional in your responses.

Over time, your mindful, attuned approach will help your child develop integration between the emotional and logical regions of his brain. As your child progresses through family therapy and EMDR and you respond at home with *Integrative Parenting* methods, he or she will heal from past traumas, develop a more secure attachment with you, think about his or her own thoughts, feelings, and behaviors, and function better at school and home.

IT'S YOUR TURN . . .

1. Look at the list of your child's most concerning behaviors and the list of triggers you started after reading Chapter 1 and add to the list of identified triggers, if you can.

2. List the situations that you think may increase your child's overall vulnerability. For example, is he more vulnerable when he is tired or hungry? Does she seem more vulnerable around the anniversary of her adoption or around her birthday?

3. Look at the list of hypothesized negative beliefs you started after reading chapter one. Add to this list if you can. What are the emotions associated with your child's beliefs?

4. Think about how you have been responding to each of your child's behaviors. What words, actions, voice tone, and body language do you use? Does your child suffer from underlying grief that may be driving some of his or her behaviors? Write down some attuned responses that you would like to implement to help calm your child's brain. Remember, it requires a great deal of practice to shift away from emotion-driven, habitual parenting responses to the more attuned *Integrative Parenting* methods.

Chapter 4

Becoming a Happier Parent

By the conclusion of this chapter, you will be able to . . .

1. Find healthy ways to lower your stress.
2. Recognize your triggers and rewire your responses.
3. Pull out your own "negative thought dominoes" and replace them with happier ones.
4. Pull out the "action dominoes" you would like to do away with and incorporate more *Integrative Parenting* habits.

Parenting is hard. Parenting children with attachment or trauma issues is megahard. By now, you are beginning to understand the *Integrative Parenting* approach and why it is effective for helping your child, but you may be asking yourself, "How can I manage my day-to-day stress and frustration so that I stop yelling and lecturing and start using more of this stuff?" You may be thinking, "Now that I know what I *should* be doing to help my child, I feel worse about myself when I don't do it."

If your energy and zest for life have "gone missing," you need to refuel your tank in some way. You may not be able to help the way you feel right now this minute, but you can make changes in your lifestyle and routine that can, over time, bring back feelings of joy and happiness you forgot existed. You may be suffering from traumatic stress due to the intense burden of raising a traumatized child and the hundreds of stressful circumstances you have found yourself in day after day. Your marriage may be suffering as a result, your friends may have moved on without you, and you may find that your world has gotten so small that it is just you and your child, stuck in an endless cycle of angry reactions.

Let your child's needs propel you to take care of your own needs for health and wellness. Think about the safety lecture you hear every time you travel by air: "Parents, in the event of an emergency, fasten your own oxygen mask first. After your mask is secure, help your child with his [or her] mask." If you have little joy in your life and you are unable to stay mindful or calm, stop and take stock. What is going on in your life and inside of you that is keeping you stuck? You deserve to feel better.

PARENT DOMINOES

Think about the domino effect described in Chapter 3. Children with a history of attachment trauma experience a cascade of falling dominoes on a regular basis. Negative perceptions lead to big feelings, which lead to big reactions, which lead to more negative responses from others, which lead to more negative thoughts and feelings, and so forth. But children are not alone in this all-too-human experience of cascading emotions, thoughts, and feelings that culminate in a loss of control. Our colleague Ann Potter (2011b) has pointed out that parents, too, are subject to loss of control following a cascade of falling dominoes. Unfortunately, when the parent's falling dominoes merge with the child's dominoes, the parent's dominoes are knocking over the child's dominoes, and the child's dominoes are knocking over the parent's dominoes until there is a riot of falling dominoes. This situation can easily result in a meltdown for both parties.

The Beginning of the Parent's Domino Effect: Vulnerability Factors

Think back to the window of tolerance described in the first chapter. Just like your child, you have a certain window of tolerance for stress within which you generally can manage what comes up and still think logically and act effectively. When the stress gets too high, however, you get overwhelmed and find yourself outside of your calm window. Your heart starts pumping hard, you start breathing rapidly, and your body is flooded with stress hormones. On the rare occasions when the stars are aligned perfectly and you have no extra challenges in your life, your tolerance window may be open especially wide, and you surprise yourself with the way in which you tackle the extra projects at work, handle the five o'clock traffic, and respond to your child's tantrum after dinner. When you are affected by a mega-dose of external stress factors, on the other hand, your window narrows. External stressors can drain your extra reserves of patience and cause you to lose your best coping skills. It is important to stay mindful of situations (in addition to the challenges you face with your child) that make you more vulnerable to your own form of meltdowns. Here are some possibilities:

- Lack of sleep, for any reason
- Pain or illness of any kind
- Recent loss of any kind
- Interpersonal conflict
- Financial worries
- Loneliness and isolation
- Working excessive hours
- Extra demands on time and resources for any reason
- Demands from other children, elderly parents, or other family members
- Major change, such as a move, a new job, or a new relationship
- Active addictions
- An emotional disorder/chemical imbalance
- Your own trauma history, including childhood experiences of abuse or neglect

Look over this list and think about which items apply to you now or may apply to you in the future. Are you coping with some external factors that are not on the list? Which of your stress factors are temporary? Changes or external demands usually come and go. Illness or pain can be temporary or chronic. Are there any vulnerability factors that need your attention? Do you have conditions for which you should get treatment, such as sleep problems, pain, illness, or addictions? Are there relationship or financial problems for which you should seek some professional help? Are there emotional issues that may be causing you to feel more vulnerable to big reactions?

We all experience some vulnerability factors that cannot be changed. However, by doing some soul-searching and incorporating some healthy self-care habits, you can create a calmer, happier, and more fulfilled life. Open your mind to the various possibilities. Yoga, meditation, or prayer can calm your brain and increase your capacity for mindful self-awareness. Walking, exercise classes, or hobbies can lower your felt stress, increase feelings of pleasure, and expand your window of tolerance. Prayer, spiritual books, study groups, or church/temple involvement can help you look deeper into the meaning and purpose of your life, increase your faith in something greater than yourself, and help you find greater serenity and optimism for life.

Interpersonal connections are vital to everyone's well-being. Adoptive and foster parents benefit from getting together with other parents. Look for support groups or adoptive or foster parent organizations in your area. If you do not have a social support network available to you, consider creating one through self-help groups, a religious organization, contacts with old friends, a book club, or a lunch group.

Don't give up on doing things that will help you feel better because you have children. Set up regular outside care for your children through a local respite service (a service that specializes in providing relief for parents of challenging children) or find trustworthy friends or relatives who are willing to help. Some parents set up respite or child care for a few hours a week or for a weekend every month. Respite gives parents needed space to recharge their energy and regain perspective. Regular respite also gives partners time to pay attention to one another and nurture their relationship.

Another option is to find a friend with children and take turns providing relief for one another. If you are without funds to help you with child care, network through support groups, neighbors, or your church/temple to find another parent who would like to trade off child care with you.

In the heat of a difficult moment with your child, it may be tempting to use respite as a threat: "I've had enough of this behavior—you're going to respite this weekend." But this type of statement will intensify your child's deep-seated fears of abandonment and worsen his behaviors over the long run. If you talk about plans for leaving him with another trusted adult as a way of giving everyone a little variety and break in routine, he will come to view respite as a normal part of the family routine. Think of respite as part of your own healthy self-care regimen.

IDENTIFYING YOUR OWN TRIGGERS

It is important to identify those child behaviors that are most triggering to you personally. For many parents, child behaviors that are viewed as signs of "disrespect" are most triggering. These challenging behaviors may include talking back, refusing to obey, using a "snotty" tone, lying, stealing, and any other acting-out behaviors. For many parents, the behaviors that are especially triggering are those behaviors that are embarrassing, such as behaving in socially unacceptable ways in public places, in school, or in the family's place of worship. Other parents are most reactive to dangerous or risky behaviors, or actions that are hurtful toward other children in the family. Some parents are most challenged by behaviors that are "gross," including regressive toileting behaviors or poor hygiene. Identify which behaviors are particularly triggering for you and make a plan for managing your own emotional reaction. Remind yourself that your child interpreted early situations to mean that it is not safe to love or be close, that others don't care about her, and that she has to be in charge of getting what she needs. Your child's skewed perceptions and her survival brain drive all of her acting-out behaviors. Although her behaviors may look strange, remind yourself that they are also the same behaviors exhibited by other children with a similar history.

PULLING OUT YOUR NEGATIVE THOUGHT DOMINOES

Parents raising children with severe behaviors naturally start questioning themselves when things are not going well. Child behaviors such as defiance, lying, sexual reactivity, or stealing naturally trigger hopeless, anxious, or angry thoughts in parents. The problem is, those negative thoughts can be dominoes that lead to emotion-driven reactions. By staying aware of your negative thoughts, you can "pull out" the negative thought dominoes and replace them with more helpful, rational thoughts.

Judgmental Thoughts

Thoughts of yourself as "bad" and your child as "bad" or "scary" are a natural reaction to your child's severe behaviors. Thoughts may include . . .

- "I'm a bad/worthless parent."
- "I have a bad/scary child."

The truth is that you are not a bad parent and this is not a bad child. Your child's behaviors may look scary, but in actuality those behaviors are driven by fear and anxiety. Your child's behaviors are manifestations of feelings and beliefs rooted in his past. Your child has a narrow window of tolerance because he operates out of his survival brain. Remind yourself of the rational, more helpful thought:

• "My child and I are both just scared inside."

Embarrassed Thoughts

It is natural to feel embarrassed by your child's behaviors. All parents are subject to embarrassment at times. Our identity is wrapped up in being a parent, and we view the child's behaviors as evidence of our success or failure in this role. Critical comments or "looks" from other parents, teachers or school staff, friends, or extended family can worsen our embarrassment. Negative thoughts may include . . .

• "This is humiliating."
• "Others are looking down at me/judging me."
• "Others think I'm a failure."

It is important to separate your child's problems from who you are as a person and as a parent. It is important to remember that you are assuming you can read others' minds, whereas they are just as likely to be viewing you with compassion and admiring how you are coping with your child's behaviors. The opinions of those who would pass judgment are not important. Remind yourself of the rational, more helpful thought:

• "Others don't have the appropriate knowledge or insight."

• "I don't need validation from others to know I am doing the right thing for my child."

Hopeless Thoughts

Hopeless thoughts are normal when stress is high. It is hard to see in that moment that there is importance or a bigger meaning to the challenges you face. It is easy to forget that there is nothing more important than changing your child's life when you yourself are operating out of your survival brain. Negative thoughts may include . . .

• "Here we go again—this will never get better."
• "My child will never heal from what happened to him."
• "I have ruined my life by adopting this child."

The truth is that all parents of children with attachment and trauma issues feel this way at times. Remind yourself that you are choosing a more meaningful life by focusing on the important task of helping your child. Expect your child to move two steps forward and one step back, and then celebrate each small step forward. Remind yourself of the rational, more helpful thought:

- "Parenting this child is important work. With the help of the therapists, over time, I can help change the course of this child's life."

Misguided "Emotion-Driven" Thoughts

If you were raised in a punitive fashion with regular scoldings and spankings, you were naturally indoctrinated with this emotion-driven approach. You have naturally incorporated your parents' methods and ways of thinking about parenting, and the *Integrative Parenting* methods feel foreign and counterintuitive to you. Stay mindful and aware of the "emotion-driven" thoughts that surface. For example . . .

- "My child needs to learn her lesson—I can't let her get away with this."
- "He is just a spoiled brat."
- "A good spanking will teach her a thing or two."
- "I need to hear him admit that he is to blame."

The truth is that your child is injured. If she needed a wheelchair or crutches to get around, it would be easier to remember that her early wounds have left her feeling unsafe, mistrustful, and alone. Remind yourself of the rational, more helpful thought:

- "My child feels unsafe in the world and needs my help to learn that he can trust me and that I will keep him safe."

Misguided Thoughts Regarding the Child's Motivations

When your child is acting out of her survival brain and is ready to fight as part of her activated nervous system, her angry face, words, and actions naturally feel like an assault to you. The emotional part of your brain is activating your fight or flight reactions. Thoughts that your child is a threat and motivated to harm are natural, including . . .

- "My child is disrespecting me."
- "My child is out to get me/hurt me."
- "My child hates me and has it in for me."

The truth is that your child's voice, words, and actions, which are coming from *his* survival brain, are triggering *your* survival brain. The truth is that your child is suffering from intense emotional pain under all that commotion. The truth is that he wants to be loved by you, but he has to push you away because his vulnerable feelings make him feel unsafe. Remind yourself of the rational, more helpful thought:

- "My child is afraid of being vulnerable, but deep down he wants to be close."

MORE DOMINOES: YOUR FEELINGS AND BODY SENSATIONS

Common emotions carried by parents of children with attachment or trauma issues include shame and guilt, anxiety, anger, frustration, powerlessness, hurt, and grief. These powerful emotions can be immediate and overwhelming. It is important that you stay mindful of your emotions and step back, breathe, and calm yourself in order to find your rational thinking mind before engaging with your child.

It is impossible to separate the emotions, the mind, and the body. Stay aware of where your emotions land in your body. If you listen to your body, it can signal you to step back and take some breaths. Just notice:

Do you feel heaviness in your chest?

Do you carry your stress in your neck or back?

Do you tend to get sick to your stomach?

Does your head hurt?

Do you get shaky?

Noticing the sensations in your body is an important part of staying mindful of your inner state and taking care of yourself before you lose control. Step back, breathe, meditate, say a prayer, or call a friend. Use the "buddy system" with your partner and relieve one another when either one of you becomes overwhelmed.

MORE DOMINOES: YOUR ACTIONS

If you analyze your own dominoes and how they merge with your child's dominoes, you will see that your thoughts, emotions, and sensations lead to your actions that trigger your child's thoughts, emotions, sensations, and actions—and vice versa. Your falling dominoes trigger your child's dominoes, and your child's dominoes trigger your dominoes. Your child's therapeutic team will try to help her pull out her dominoes by changing her thoughts and feelings and learning new behavioral skills. At the same time, it will be important for you to remove as many dominoes as you can by staying aware of your vulnerabilities, triggers, thoughts, and feelings, and practicing positive self-talk and new behavioral responses. Remember that your angry face, tone, and actions light up the emotional centers in your child's brain. Taking care of your side of the street by changing your face, voice, gestures, words, and actions will change the entire trajectory of your interactions.

Make a conscious commitment to stay mindful of the volume and tone of your voice, the look on your face, and your body posture. The next time your child acts out in some way, ask yourself:

Am I clenching my jaw?
Am I leaning over my child?
Am I furrowing my brow or narrowing my eyes?
Is my voice loud or harsh?

If you can "catch yourself," stop and take a deep breath. Walk away for a moment. Find a phrase or "mantra" that you can use on a regular basis. A *mantra* is a word or phrase that you find uplifting or inspiring. For example, a mantra might be, "Let go, let God," or the words, "One day at a time." Write your mantra on sticky notes and place them on your bedroom mirror, on the refrigerator, and in the car. Make your mantra a password on your computer. Don't expect yourself to be perfect, but with practice, you can use your mantra, perhaps with a deep breath and a long, slow exhalation, to calm yourself. Come back to the situation and try again. Switch to an *Integrative Parenting* approach by lowering your voice, softening your face, and attuning to your child's underlying feelings and thoughts. Remember that it cannot happen overnight, but over time, the *Integrative Parenting* strategies in conjunction with the therapy will help your child heal.

YOUR DOMINOES AND YOUR CHILD'S MELTDOWNS

In a full-blown "downstairs" meltdown, your child may scream names and obscenities, hit, kick, throw things, and even try to bite. These behaviors can certainly be shocking, and your natural feelings in response may be hurt, anger, anxiety, fear, helplessness, and hopelessness. As we noted above, your automatic negative thoughts may pop up with "I'm a failure," "My child is bad," and "This is hopeless." In response to the upset emotions and negative thoughts, you may react with angry attempts to control your child or to push your child away. You may react with behaviors similar to your child's behaviors, such as screaming, punching things, throwing things, or hitting the child. All of these types of parent behaviors become dominoes that fuel the child's meltdown. Even if you yell loud enough to frighten your child out of his meltdown in the moment, it will stop it only temporarily and increase his instability in the long run.

You may be wondering what you can do with your own emotions in the moment. The first step is to stay mindfully aware of your own inner state and immediately begin breathing slowly, from your diaphragm. Remind yourself not to take it personally. Your child's logical brain is not operational right now, and she is likely in a much younger state of mind. Remember that this is a temporary situation and that if you "ride the wave," it will pass. Memorize words that will be most calming to your child—for example:

> "You're having some big feelings. I'll give you some space to cool down, but I won't go away. I'll be right here."

Whereas a downstairs meltdown is about loss of control and panic feelings rooted in the past, your child's upstairs meltdown has a goal. Your child is in survival brain, and in the moment, she believes that she must do everything she can to get you to give her what she wants. Concentrate on your breath. Remember that it's not personal. Your child believes that she must demand to get what she wants because of early unmet needs. Giving in or reacting with anger will reinforce your child's survival brain. By staying mindful, you can take a firm stance while staying calm.

STRENGTHENING CONNECTION IN THE AFTERMATH

Parent dominoes can fuel all types of acting-out behaviors. By staying aware of your thoughts and feelings, practicing rational self-talk, using positive mantras, and breathing from the diaphragm, you can stay in your "calm window" and think about what to do with your logical brain intact.

After your child acts out in some way, remind yourself that reconnection and repair will help build your relationship with your child. Many parents worry that affection and love shown in the aftermath of a crisis will reinforce the child's negative behavior. They believe they must give the child "the silent treatment" to "teach him [her] a lesson." This could not be further from the truth.

The most effective response is the *Integrative Parenting* approach of connection and repair. Words that calm the child's survival brain and help increase attachment security and stabilize behaviors include:

- "I love you."
- "You are OK."
- "We are still connected."
- "We are always connected."

Taking the time to be emotionally and physically present with your child following any type of acting out will strengthen your child's ability to operate out of his logical brain as he moves forward. Any time you are able to reach out to your child when he is feeling badly and pull him closer is an opportunity for forging your relationship and strengthening your child's brain. You might find that during this reconnection phase, you and your child are able to talk at a deeper level about the things that are bothering him. Through these connecting experiences, over time, your child will become more securely attached, which will calm his brain, widen his window of tolerance, and allow him to think and process more normally.

DAVID AND HIS MOM: INTERSECTING DOMINOES

In this example, David's mom is completely unaware that her dominoes are intersecting with David's dominoes. As David's actions get triggered, he in turn triggers his mom, and the situation rapidly escalates out of control. Because the cycle reinforces negative thoughts and feelings in both of them, a recurrence is likely.

Nine-year-old David enters the house after school, like many children, tired from the day and famished. David's mom, still annoyed that David left his bed unmade that morning, tells David to make his bed and get his homework started without making any kind of emotional or physical connection with him. David becomes overwhelmed and reacts with anger. David's mom feels disrespected and reacts in a punitive manner. David feels attacked and begins losing control of his emotions and his body. His mom feels like a failure as a mother and even more reactive to David. David escalates into a full-fledged "downstairs" meltdown and winds up knocking over a lamp when he throws a pillow. Furious now, his mom drags him into his room and leaves him there, then sinks into the couch with a headache. Alone in his room, David shouts with frustration and then sobs in despair, all alone. There is no reconnection between them. Both David and his mom are left feeling rejected, ashamed, and angry.

This scenario may have left you with a headache, but it may help you understand how the parent's dominoes can set the child's dominoes in action, and vice versa, until both sets of dominoes are banging into one another.

Let's sort it all out. First, what factors made David's mom more vulnerable to getting triggered?

1. David's mom was tired from working all day.
2. She was annoyed that David hadn't made his bed that morning.

David also was suffering from some vulnerability factors:

1. David was tired.
2. He was hungry.

We can also assume, if David has a history of attachment trauma, that he is sensitive to feelings of rejection, has difficulty trusting that adults are on his side, and is easily stressed by school and homework. Figure 4.1 illustrates the chain of dominoes, each one leading to the next one, and culminating in David's giant meltdown.

As you examine the dominoes of thoughts, feelings, and behaviors (Mom's and David's) in Figure 4.1, think about how David's mom might be able to "pull some dominoes" from her cascade of falling dominoes the next time. First, David's mom could increase her mindful self-awareness and attunement to David by reminding herself that they are both naturally hungry and tired at the end of every work/school day and that they are both likely to have a shrunken window of tolerance. David's mom can develop a plan to sit down with David as soon as he gets home to share a snack and reconnect with one another after their day. If later, David still

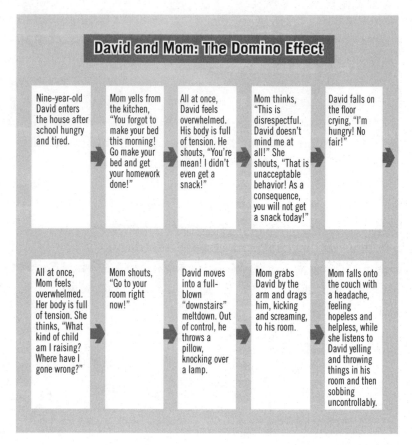

FIGURE 4.1. The "domino effect" illustrates how David's mother's dominos intersected with David's dominos, escalating David's survival brain to produce his meltdown. Identify where David's mother might have "pulled a domino" and changed the outcome.

whines about his homework, his mom could make a point to listen and ask about what is hard or frustrating for him. If David has a meltdown at some point anyway, his mom could give him space but stay close. She could move in and provide reassurance when he is ready, thereby shortening the episode and utilizing the opportunity to strengthen his sense of security in their relationship.

COUPLE ISSUES

Staying connected as a couple can be a real challenge when partners are raising a child with trauma and attachment problems. Each partner is looking to the other for support, for reassurance, and for answers, and each parent simultaneously feels emotionally depleted and unable to be supportive to the other. In addition, parents often come from different backgrounds and have different styles of parenting, and yet neither parent may be feeling successful due to a lack of knowledge regarding attachment trauma. Naturally, parents easily fall into patterns of arguing.

Reading this book together may help you and your partner "get on the same page" in responding to your child. This may be a "new page" in your lives. It is also important to sit down together and talk about how you can support one another and how you can keep your relationship strong despite the stress in your household. Make date nights a priority, with help from a respite provider, family, or friend. Make it a point to talk and share each day after the children are in bed, or make lunch dates together on school days. A stronger relationship between the two of you will increase your resilience as individuals and will provide a more secure environment for your child. Experts tell us that children do better overall when their parents are happy with one another (Gottman & DeClaire, 2001, p. 22). If there is too much conflict for the two of you to improve your relationship on your own, ask your child's therapeutic team to refer you to a counselor who is trained and experienced in helping couples and who has a basic understanding of the *Integrative Parenting* approach.

EXTENDED FAMILY ISSUES

Many families participating in treatment at our center experience conflict with extended family members in regard to the child with attachment and trauma issues. Frequently, because extended family members do not understand the effects of past trauma on a child's neurology, belief system, and emotional development, they blame the child's current parents for the child's behaviors. Extended family members may give the parents directives such as, "Give him a good spanking," "Stop spoiling her," or "Teach him some manners." The extended family may tell the parents to place the child elsewhere, remove the child from her medications, or give the child more medications. Extended family members sometimes admonish parents for adopting the child. When children act out only in the nuclear family, other relatives may even accuse the parent of exaggerating the child's behavioral problems.

If you are struggling with self-doubt due to the numerous challenges that you face every day, you may be more vulnerable to criticism, especially from your parents and extended family members. If your parents or other family members are critical or rejecting of your children, it is natural to feel hurt, defensive, and sad.

It may be helpful to give extended family members this book to read, or it may be helpful to sit down and talk directly with them about how they can be helpful. Remind yourself that *you* are the child's parent, that you are doing everything you can to help your child, and that your extended family members simply do not understand. You may want to develop some responses that you can use when the other family members make comments. For example:

- "Sis, I know you are coming from a place of care and concern for us, but I want to reassure you that we have some good support and advice that we are following."
- "Mom, I know it is hard to understand, but your grandchild came to us with some emotional injuries that we are trying to heal. It would be most helpful to me if you could try to stay positive."

GRIEF ISSUES

Many parents do not realize that they are suffering from grief. You may be grieving due to losses you have experienced since your child joined your family. You may be grieving loss of control, loss of alone time, time with friends, or couple time. You may be unresolved about earlier infertility issues. You may be mourning the child you had imagined raising and grieving due to the challenges faced by the other children in your family. Give some serious consideration to talking with a therapist of your own to help you work through your feelings of grief and loss. An individual therapist, perhaps one who uses EMDR with adults, can help you remove the obstacles to finding acceptance for life on life's terms, enjoying your child's unique traits, and finding meaning and accomplishment in the small steps.

TAKE CARE OF YOUR OWN PAST

Often, parents don't recognize how their own past may be playing out in their relationship with their children. Even when parents have a birth child, the experience of parenting can trigger childhood memories in parents—consciously or subconsciously. Sitting down to dinner with your children may trigger the best and the worst memories of sitting down to dinner with your parents when you were young. Watching your child march off to school may trigger memories of your favorite teachers or your worst teachers. Watching your child enjoy his 9th birthday party will likely trigger memories related to turning 9. If you have a large number of distressing childhood memories, feelings of distress are likely to surface, consciously or subconsciously.

Raising difficult children is particularly triggering for parents who hold painful childhood memories (Wesselmann, 1998). It is natural for parents to experience sudden feelings of confusion, rejection, hurt, and anger as their children demand attention and simultaneously push their parents away. The present-day emotions tap into earlier life experiences of confusion, rejection, hurt, and anger. The triggered emotional memories of the past can quickly push parents beyond their window of tolerance into survival mode. Think a little more in depth about your childhood . . .

- Did you consider your parents warm and loving?
- Was it an environment where you could share your feelings openly?
- Could you talk about things that troubled you?

If these conditions were true for you, *Integrative Parenting* will come more naturally to you. On the other hand . . .

- Did you grow up in a home where children were to be seen and not heard?
- Were your problems dismissed as unimportant?
- Were you criticized, rejected, or shamed?

If these conditions were true for you, you may not have had anyone to help you verbalize your thoughts and feelings. You may have been forced to cope by shutting down. Now it may be difficult for you to tune into your own feelings and thoughts, let alone imagine the feelings and thoughts your child is experiencing.

If no one ever hugged you or held you when you were a child, physical affection toward your child now may feel awkward. If anger was toxic and explosive in your childhood home, the expression of anger by anyone may trigger intense emotional and physical reactions now that are hard for you to control. If you felt unloved as a child, the push–pull you experience from your child may feel intensely threatening.

The Inner Child and You

Your child carries a traumatized, hurt younger child self on the inside. Current situations that tap into old feelings of hurt, fear, shame, or anger take your child to an emotional state she lived in at a younger age. The challenging behaviors of your child's "inner child" will, in turn, trigger any old, buried hurts and fears that you may carry. Her meltdowns, defiance, stealing, and lying will trigger any fears of abandonment or feelings of rejection that you may have felt as a child. Essentially, the "inner (younger) child" within your child will trigger the hurt "inner child" within you. If you find yourself reacting at times in ways that surprise and embarrass you—if you feel like you are not always in control of your reactions and behaviors, but watching yourself from the sidelines—your inner child is likely activated. Remember—you are far from alone. Many parents share your experience and find it extremely difficult to stay in a rational adult state and avoid their own "hurt child" feelings and thoughts in the face of the push–pull behaviors of their children.

DOING YOUR OWN THERAPY

When your own feelings and personal experiences prevent you from carrying out *Integrative Parenting* strategies or get in the way of supporting your child during integrative Team Treatment, you may benefit from working with a therapist one on one. Many of the parents of traumatized children involved in therapy at our center have found working with their own EMDR therapist to be life-changing.

In a book for laypeople entitled *Getting Past Your Past*, Shapiro (2012) writes: "Reactions that seem irrational are often exactly that. But irrational doesn't mean that there is no reason for them. . . . The automatic reactions that control our emotions come from neural associations with our memory networks that are independent of our higher reasoning power" (p. 9). EMDR reaches the stored "stuck" experiences, emotions, and reactions and integrates the upsetting material with stored adaptive, positive information. Whether you choose to work with an EMDR therapist, attend talk therapy, or participate in a therapy group, you deserve to heal and feel better so that you can experience greater joy and happiness in your life. You deserve to become a happier parent.

Your child's therapeutic team is there to help you. Feel free to ask them for a referral to a therapist. They will be happy to help you find just the right therapist who is a good match for your personality and your needs.

IT'S YOUR TURN . . .

1. At the top of one of the pages of your notebook write "Self-Care." List activities or changes you can commit to incorporating into your life to help you recharge. Your list may include a variety of ideas, such as making a lunch date with a friend each week, joining a spiritual group, joining a book club, attending counseling for yourself, finding child-care help, joining an exercise class, or practicing meditation. There may be certain people, places, or activities that are creating unhappiness for you that you need to remove from your life in order to feel better. Remember, in order to feel better it is vital to make some changes in your lifestyle. Start making your changes immediately. Don't waste any time. You deserve to feel better today.

2. Write the word "Triggers" at the top of the next page and list those situations with which you struggle the most.

3. Write "Negative Thoughts" and "Helpful Thoughts" at the top of the next page, and list the upsetting thoughts that tend to crop up when you get triggered, such as "My child is bad," "I'm a failure," or "I'm a bad parent." Following each negative thought, write rational, more helpful thoughts you can use to dispute the negative ones, such as, "My child's behaviors are driven by trauma," "Nobody is perfect," "I'm a good person," and "I'm continuing to grow and learn." This exercise will help you pull out the negative thought dominoes and become more mindful and positive in your thinking.

4. At the top of another page, write "Integrative Parenting." Write down the changes you plan to make in your responses to your child's behaviors.

Chapter 5

Boundaries and Consequences with Love and Attunement

By the conclusion of this chapter, you will be able to . . .

1. Avoid emotion-driven parent responses that are damaging to attachment security.
2. Sort out which of your child's behaviors belong in the "small stuff" basket and require a minimal response for the most effective outcome.
3. Develop a reward system that will be most effective for some of your child's specific behaviors.
4. Enhance your relationship with your child by using consequences the integrative way.

Although children with a history of attachment loss or hurt have a special need for emotional attunement and experiences of connection and closeness, they also need structure, rules, and boundaries, like other children. Sometimes children have no motivation for making good choices. Sometimes children don't know the appropriate ways to behave. The trick for managing your child's behaviors day-to-day is figuring out how to supply the proper boundaries and teach the appropriate behaviors while simultaneously strengthening the relationship.

DISCIPLINE—A TRICKY TASK

Disciplining the child with early trauma and attachment wounds is a tricky endeavor. Your child learned to mistrust adults very early in life. Because deep down he believes it is not safe to be close to you or go to you for comfort, he also cannot trust you to be in charge.

You do need concrete strategies to help manage your child's behaviors day-to-day. Your child needs help learning what is appropriate and what is not appropriate. However, the methods that will be most effective with your child will not look like methods your parents used when they were raising you, and they may be different from the way you are raising other children in your home. The more emotion-driven your responses, the less effective you will be. Emotion-driven parenting tends to involve scolding, yelling, lecturing, shaming, and repeated punishments, which reinforce the child's belief, "You are mean and I am bad." Wounded children who are parented this way cope by turning off their vulnerable feelings and convincing themselves they do not care. Wounded children learn not to care about how many sentences they have to write, how many days they are grounded, or how many spankings they get. At the same time, the punishments and scoldings reinforce the children's mistrust, hypervigilance, and reactivity. Old-school punishments may result in short-term compliance, but compliance driven by fear is merely superficial and doesn't last.

Remember that if you use emotion-driven strategies, you will stop your child's behaviors in the moment, but worsen her behaviors in the long run. Her fears and mistrust will escalate as your emotions escalate. You may stop her behavior with force today, but you will have thrown salt onto the attachment wound. The future will only be worse for everyone.

THE "HOW NOT TO . . . "

Like the "how," the "how not to" refers to the way you carry things out and the kind of environment you create. The following sections cover the basic ingredients in a recipe for disaster when it comes to managing children with trauma and attachment issues. These methods trigger the most negative beliefs of traumatized children and are likely to activate the hurt younger child self within. Every one of these parent actions is emotion-driven and will render every behavior management strategy null and void.

Lecturing

Lecturing usually involves a stern voice, a stern look, and little participation on the part of the child except for occasional head nods and resentful grunts. The recipient of the lecture is most likely not feeling connected, good about the relationship, or good about himself.

Yelling

Any recipient of another's raised voice generally feels threatened. Children with a history of attachment trauma are immediately triggered into a hyper-aroused state in which they cannot process information or control their emotions and behaviors.

Sarcasm

You know that any debate or argument has become personal in nature when the participants begin using sarcasm. Sarcasm is never helpful in finding a solution for any two people, and it always results in hurt feelings. Parents who are not mindful of their own emotions and behaviors are easily triggered to using sarcasm, which triggers their children to increased feelings of hurt, mistrust, and anger.

Shaming

One father said:

> "I thought it was my job to talk sense into Cameron. I thought if could just make Cameron see what he had done wrong, and make him feel guilty about it, he would stop doing some of the crazy lying and stealing. But the more I scolded, the more he shut down. It just drove the wedge between us deeper. I had to learn to stop shaming and just focus on building our relationship—and give the therapy a chance. Now I feel like things are finally getting better between Cameron and me."

You may have found yourself scolding until you were blue in the face, in an attempt to make your child understand what she did wrong, feel remorseful, and admit her wrongdoing. You probably felt more and more frustrated and over-wrought as the conversation continued—and defeated and despairing when nothing changed.

Escalating Punishments/Consequences

One mother sat down with us to talk about the possibility of her children attending treatment at our center, and we inquired if her children would be all right in the waiting room while we talked. She said, "They will be fine—they are in the middle of writing 5,000 sentences each." This mother was trapped in a cycle of escalating punishments. The fact is, the bigger the punishment, the more the punishment reinforces the child's belief, "My parent is mean, and I am bad." Because the punishments match the belief system of these children, nothing changes within them. They resign themselves to a life of punishment after punishment, because they believe it is the only life that they can have. They have no motivation to try to do things differently—they believe there is no other way. If they came out of an early situation that was abusive, a life full of negative feelings about themselves, others, and the world is the only life they know.

Spanking

You may have been spanked. You may have spanked other children with no harm done. Your neighbors may spank. And yes, spanking usually stops the misbehavior immediately. But please, *don't spank*. The research shows clearly that children who are spanked regularly become more aggressive over time—even when the spankings appear to be effective in the moment. The positive effect lasts only for as long as the child is fearful. When the acute fear wears off, the aftereffects include increased hypervigilance, hyperarousal, and reactivity—hence, increased aggression in the long run. Many parents of traumatized children report that the children "seem to want to be spanked." They push and push until parents finally spank them, and then they "appear fine." Children who have been physically abused expect to be spanked and hate the feeling of waiting around for it. They feel much more in control when they can force it to happen—and if they have always been spanked, it simply feels right. Once it happens, they don't have to wait for it—until the next time they get the feeling that they are waiting for it. Spanking fuels aggression in the long run and does nothing for brain integration.

Figure 5.1 is a visual summary of emotion-driven parenting, in which anger is at the foundation and attunement is minimal. This style reinforces children's negative beliefs about themselves and their parents, causes further damage to the attachment relationship, and exacerbates the survival brain.

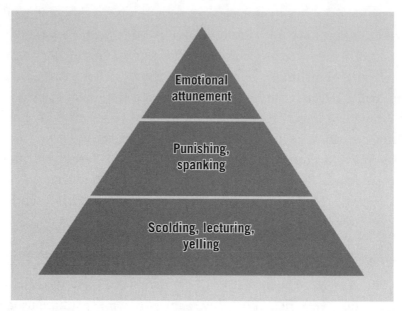

FIGURE 5.1. The "emotion-driven parenting" matrix illustrates how parents discipline their children when they react automatically, out of anger. Children already in survival mode remain poorly connected and hyperaroused.

THE "HOW"

There are numerous parenting programs that describe various behavior management techniques. Any behavior management system may have useful ideas that can be effective if parents carry out the technique with an emotionally attuned, relationship-oriented attitude. In other words, there is nothing more important than the "how." The "how" refers to the way you carry things out as you implement the particular strategies, as well as the type of environment you create. If you follow the "how" when implementing the "what," your behavior management strategies will avoid damaging the relationship between you and your child—despite your child's fears related to trust and closeness. In fact, implementing the behavior management strategies with the right attitudes and environmental conditions can actually strengthen your relationship with your traumatized child and help strengthen her thinking brain—while teaching her the correct ways to behave. On the other hand, if the "how" skills are missing, any parenting strategy you try is bound to fail if you are parenting a child with trauma and attachment issues.

By now, the *Integrative Parenting* "how" strategies should make perfect sense. There will be no surprises here, so we keep these sections brief.

Stay Emotionally Attuned

Look beyond your child's behavior and remember the core mistrust and negative beliefs about self, others, and life that are driving the behaviors. Emotional attunement may consist of observations such as, "I know it's hard to be 10" or "I want to understand more about what you are going through." Emotional attunement may consist of a hug or an offer of a back rub. Remember that your child has a very mixed-up brain and intense feelings he does not understand. Attuning emotionally with your child following a behavior will give your child the connection he needs to be able to reflect upon his own feelings, thoughts, and actions. If you need to correct your child in some way, take the time to attune emotionally first in order to help your child feel loved. This will help him avoid painful feelings carried by his inner child, such as shame, mistrust, and anxiety. Even if you believe that your child needs a consequence of some kind as motivation for change, you can avoid losing the emotional connection and help him view the consequence as a way to help him, not hurt him. Attunement will enhance the effectiveness of any disciplinary strategy you decide to implement, whether you are removing privileges or asking him to sit quietly for a few minutes.

Stay Calm

Throughout any interaction, stay aware of your own emotional state and use your skills for self-calming. Staying within your own window of tolerance is key to keeping your child within hers. If she stays in her calm window, she will be more capable of using her logical thinking brain and listening to your sensible ideas. Use a matter-of-fact tone of voice, without sarcasm or anger, and use a logical approach to solving the difficulties. The more you model logical problem-solving, thinking things through, and staying calm, the more your child will learn from her mistakes.

Find Ways to Connect

Notice when your child is dysregulated and connect, connect, *connect*. Even before your child becomes dysregulated, find a way to connect. Remember that when you connect with your child, you are automatically regulating him. Think about the metaphor of the hot air balloon. As your child begins to ramp up, or before he even begins to ramp up, your connection with him becomes the tether that keeps him grounded. Take a moment to touch, make eye contact, and talk multiple times every single day. A hand on the shoulder, a cuddle, a quick shoulder rub, a joke, or a funny story all can become methods of connecting. Younger children often need intense physical connection to help them feel truly secure. Bundling the child up and rocking him provides rhythm and movement along with the human connection to help with neurological regulation. Rolling around on the ground with your younger child and wrestling in a fun and playful way or giving your child a big bear hug and swaying him side to side are other ways to provide neurological regulation and secure physical connection. Verbal affirmations will give your child a sense of self-worth while providing connection. Simply tell him you love him, mention something you appreciate about him, or tell him you think he is lovable and special.

Don't miss opportunities to connect—when your child comes to you with a problem or just feels talkative, turn off your cell phone or put down the dishtowel and listen. If you consistently work at keeping the feeling of connection as strong as possible between you and your child, then her missteps won't have to turn into crises. Think of every problem behavior as a potential opportunity to learn more about the emotions and upset thoughts with which your child is struggling. Verbal or physical reassurance that you are still there for her will allow your child to stay open to the conversation.

"Don't Sweat the Small Stuff"

If you are find yourself constantly correcting and constantly redirecting—and talking, talking, talking about every misbehavior, you will quickly reach a threshold at which it all loses its effectiveness. If every time your child misbehaves, you try to make him admit to what he has done and understand why his behavior is wrong, you will wind up frustrated and overwrought—and all of the attention your child is receiving will only reinforce the behavior. Furthermore, when you become worked up over your child's behavior, he will view the behavior as a problem only because it is a problem for *you*. Practice staying calm and using the fewest words you can to address the behavior, and then walking away and getting busy with something else. This approach turns the problem over to your child and avoids reinforcing the behavior with a lot of focus and attention.

Think about your child's problematic behaviors and prioritize them. Put the low-priority behaviors in the "small stuff" basket. Then choose a few more behaviors to throw in the basket. Choose not to put any energy into the small stuff behaviors. When you see a behavior that belongs in the small stuff basket, either ignore it completely (e.g., whining or complaining behaviors), or make a very small comment that makes it clear that her behavior is her problem, not yours. You want to convey that the only reason you are saying anything to her about it is because you care about her.

Provide a Structured, Predictable, Safe Environment

Attunement does not mean that "anything goes." Children with a chaotic history do far better when there is an established, predictable structure with well-defined but reasonable rules and expectations. Consistent expectations include sensible rules about everyday life such as bedtime, chores, and homework.

Be clear: *Rules that are ambiguous create anxiety.* The child with a trauma history feels stress and anxiety every time the rules change. If you act as if a certain behavior is OK one day but punishable the next, your child's anxiety will skyrocket. If you find yourself saying no, but later giving in to keep the peace (and not because you have truly changed your mind), practice tolerating the whining and begging. Keep a kind face, but give your child the message that "No really means *no*." Practice this consistently, and over time, the whining and begging will gradually lessen.

When your child breaks a rule, point it out by just "noticing" it. For example: "Sweetheart, I notice you left your shoes in the middle of the floor." Use a pleasant tone of voice to redirect: "Remember the rule—shoes in the closet." Then make sure your child follows through so she knows you mean what you say.

A home is predictable and safe only if it is free of excessive conflict. Even children with a fine early childhood become anxious when their parents fight. The child with a trauma history becomes stressed and anxious if there is a high level of conflict between her parents about childrearing or anything else, and her anxiety escalates when the conflict is intense. If there is high conflict in your relationship, seek help from a professional to work it out. You will benefit and your child will benefit.

THE "WHAT"

The "how" skills are vital, but parents still need to have some solid, reliable interventions on hand that can help prevent and interrupt difficult acting-out child behaviors on the spot. The *Integrative Parenting* "what" strategies are designed to help you teach your child appropriate behaviors and to motivate him to try, while strengthening his "thinking brain" and maintaining the feeling of connection between you. Without forgetting the very important "how," parents can implement these *Integrative Parenting* strategies again and again for "big" behaviors as well as for niggling "small" behaviors.

Preteach ("An Ounce of Prevention Is Worth a Pound of Cure")

Most parents get to know their children fairly well and are able to predict—when they think about it—which daily life events are going to be a struggle for their children. Every child has his or her own unique challenges, but most children with a history of attachment trauma share some typical difficulties. Which of these situations almost begs your child to become overstimulated or lose control in some way?

- Holidays and other special days
- Long car rides
- Visitors
- Parent talking on the phone
- Waiting rooms
- Checkout lanes stocked with enticing candy and toys
- Restaurants, especially fancy ones
- Other children over to play
- Visiting someone else's house

Preteaching is not the same as threatening. The admonition "Don't you dare act up in the waiting room, today—I expect you to be on your best behavior" is not preteaching. Preteaching is most effective when it is done with empathy for how challenging the situation feels to the child, and actually talking with the child about how to manage the situation. If you include role-playing and make it fun, you will have even more success.

Another preteaching strategy involves sitting down with your child and going over the "house rules." Explain the reasons for the various rules, and post them on the refrigerator so there can be no mistake. In the next example Becca's mom uses preteaching with her before a playdate.

Mom: Becca, I'll bet you are really looking forward to Sarah coming, aren't you? *(Becca nods.)* I would love to help you have even more fun than usual with Sarah. I know sometimes when Sarah is here, it is really hard not to fight, because you don't always want to play the same things Sarah wants to play. [Here the mom is empathizing to establish the connection before preteaching.]

Becca: Yeah, she always wants to play house, and I hate playing house. I want to play school.

Mom: Mmm-hmm. It's hard to work things out sometimes. Do you know what the word *compromise* means?

Becca: Yeah, it's when you let the other person get to choose.

Mom: Well, no, that's not it. It means you talk, and you work out a plan where you each get part of what you want. Like, for instance, we play what you want half the time and we play what I want half the time. Let's practice working out a plan. I'll be Sarah . . . *(Mom role-plays with Becca and coaches her on how to work out a compromise with Sarah.)*

Children with a history of attachment trauma are way behind their peers in social and emotional skills. Every time you teach, model, practice, and role-play with your child, you are helping your child get back on track developmentally. If you find that every time you attempt to preteach it turns out badly, the negative patterns may be too entrenched, and you will need to ask your child's therapist to help you with some preteaching in the therapist's office until you and your child can have a positive interaction.

Teach After the Fact

Poor choices and behaviors can be used as teaching moments as long as any upset is calmed down—on the part of both the child and the parents. Teaching does not mean lecturing, and avoid saying "I told you so." Use a calm, matter-of-fact tone as you explain why the behavior was unacceptable or against the rules and explain or model the preferred behavior and the reasoning behind the rules. Remember that your child lacks cause-and-effect thinking and lacks insight into why things are the way they are. Stay mindful and calm, even if you have to "fake it 'til you make it." Get the child's attention, not by raising your voice, but by getting down on his or her level if young, using a very quiet voice (but not threateningly quiet) and eye contact. When your child is dysregulated, don't even think about doing any teaching—there is no rush. For the moment, stay reassuring and calm, or if necessary, as calmly as possible, move your child to a safe place away from any triggers. A matter-of-fact discussion about what happened can take place much later, when you and your child are both inside your window of tolerance. Remember that every time you help your child problem-solve around an emotional event, you are promoting healthy brain integration. In the following vignette, Steven's parents make use of an opportunity to teach after the fact.

Eight-year-old Steven's parents were embarrassed when he became reactive to his grandmother at dinner over a serving of peas. Dad touched Steven's hand and whispered, "Take a deep breath. Remember, we talk with one another to work out our problems." Steven remained agitated but did not melt down. That night, when Steven was in bed, his dad sat down on the bed and went over the event:

> "Steven, I know you don't like peas, and you felt upset when Grandma asked you to eat your peas. Let's come up with a plan for what you can say to Grandma next time."

Together, they talked about how Steven could mention that peas are "not my favorite," and ask, "Would it be OK if I just try a small bite?" At the end, his dad praised Steven for working on a plan and using his "smart thinking brain."

Effective parents are teachers. Don't expect to teach any concept just one time. *Integrative Parenting* involves pre-teaching, teaching, and re-teaching. New ideas and new behaviors require time and repetition. You will teach and your child will learn through many examples, mistakes, and challenging situations. Remember that your child will comprehend and retain new ideas only when you and she are both in the calm window.

Put on Your "Detective's Hat"

Unlike teaching after the fact, detective work involves collaborating together to uncover the thoughts and feelings that led up to the problem behavior. After a meltdown or some type of acting-out behavior, when everything is all over and your child is calm, try saying, "Let's put on our detective hats and figure out what happened." Let your child know that you just want to help, and you want to understand more about his or her thoughts and feelings, and maybe what acted as the trigger. If you believe you were a trigger, ask your child what you could have done differently. The important thing about detective work is to keep it a collaborative effort. If your child becomes defensive and angry, let it go until your child's next therapy session. Your child's treatment team can take the lead in uncovering exactly how the dominoes fell and working to alleviate future triggers. In the following conversation, Rhonda's mother engages her 7-year-old daughter in some detective work.

Mom: *(First gives Rhonda a hug to connect with her.)* Rhonda, you were really struggling in church today, and I feel badly that we didn't have a good time together. Let's put on our detective hats and see if we can figure out what went wrong.

Rhonda: I don't know, I guess I just got mad.

Mom: Yes, you did get mad, didn't you? I wonder, what triggered your mad feelings today?

Rhonda: I think I didn't like it that Lori was sitting on your lap at church.

Mom: Oh, you didn't like Lori sitting on my lap. But that was before the service started. Were you holding in mad feelings all that time?

Rhonda: Well, and then you had your arm around her.

Mom: Oh, then I had my arm around her? So were you thinking I didn't love you, and I loved her because I had my arm around her then?

Rhonda: *(Crying now)* Yes, I always think you love her more. She's always good, and I'm always bad.

Mom: Rhonda, I love you so much. I love you both. Come here, let's snuggle a little bit and talk about how you can tell me next time you start feeling unloved.

Connect and Redirect

Siegel and Bryson (2011) encourage all parents to connect with their children prior to a redirection to promote healthy brain functioning through integration of the emotional and logical regions of the brain. Think of it this way: When you reach out and connect in some way with your child, you are lighting up the positive emotions in his right brain. When you reason with him and explain what you want him to do or not do, you are lighting up his logical left brain. By lighting up the two together, you are helping create new neural connections between right and left portions of the brain.

Because you are observing your child engage in a behavior that you want her to stop or change, you will want to connect with her quickly. A quick connection can be achieved through an empathic statement, such as, "It's hard to be a kid." A connection can be achieved through a quick hug, a light touch on the arm, or by asking your child to come and sit close. The connection can also be quickly achieved through verbal affirmations such as "Remember, I love you" or "You know, you are really special."

Redirection can be accomplished by simply noticing the child's behavior verbally and then by either expressing your concern or simply reminding him of the rule. If your child has difficulty listening or processing information, you will want to ask him for confirmation that he understands or ask him to repeat the rule out loud. In the next example, one mom, Lorilynn, forgets to connect/redirect effectively, whereas the other mom, Susan, connects and then redirects.

Lorilynn: Henry, get in here right now and pick up these toys. How many times do I have to tell you? I'm getting sick and tired of it.

Henry: *(Immediately triggered by his mother's angry voice and words, he falls into a meltdown on the floor.)*

In contrast, Susan connects and then redirects:

Susan: Honey *(giving Danny a quick hug)*, I notice that your toys are still on the floor. Remember the rule for when you finish playing with your toys? [Next, Susan redirects.] Please pick up your toys now. *(Waits for Danny to give a nod and start his job before she leaves the room.)*

Lorilynn again forgets to connect/redirect effectively:

Lorilynn: Henry, you are being too loud and bothering everybody. Stop trying to be the center of attention!

Henry: *(Immediately triggered by the anger and criticism, he becomes louder and more dysregulated.)*

Susan connects and then redirects:

Susan: I love you, Danny. Hey, come here a minute, I want to talk to you just a second. I notice that your voice is very loud right now, and I'm concerned it may disturb the other people here in the restaurant. Please practice using your inside voice—like this *(speaks softly to demonstrate)*. OK, can you do it? Let me hear you try.

Use Consequences the *Integrative* Way

The use of a consequence for each misbehavior is overkill, as your child will feel hopeless and shut down. But it is OK to give your child consequences when she is repeating a serious behavior again and again, despite teaching and redirecting. The purpose of enforcing consequences is to provide motivation for behavior change. Preteach with your child and explain that parents give consequences to help their children remember the rules. Keep the consequences light. There is generally no need to give a consequence that lasts over a day. Many parents believe that the severity of the consequence is equal to its effectiveness. Nothing could be further from the truth. The harsher the consequence, the more it reinforces the child's feelings of alienation, worthlessness, fear, and hopelessness—thereby automatically narrowing of the child's window of tolerance. Harsh consequences reinforce the child's negative beliefs, such as, "I'm bad," "I don't belong," "I'm unlovable," "Bad things always happen to me," "It's not safe to love or be close" or "Parents are mean." So be reasonable with your consequences and give your child a fresh start each day.

Cline and Faye recommend delivering consequences with empathy (1990, pp. 96–99). Most parents naturally deliver consequences in an angry state of mind. Many parents intuitively believe that their anger increases the effectiveness of the consequence. In fact, many parents believe their anger *is* the consequence. Biological children who have a solid foundation of attachment security can tolerate their parents' anger more easily. But your child may experience your anger as dangerous and triggering, lighting up his survival brain and preventing him from reflecting upon his own behavior. On the other hand, anger may be a type of reinforcement to your child, because it may be the only kind of attention he got when he was younger, or he may believe that it is the only kind of attention that he deserves.

Empathy is a powerful tool for creating a trusting relationship with your child. Empathy will help your child stay within her window of tolerance and keep her connected with you, even if you are pointing out a rule and the consequence for breaking the rule. Your empathy delivers the message "I care about you and don't want you to suffer," even as you then present the consequence. When your child feels connected and regulated, she has the capacity to learn from her mistake and to actually feel a sense of remorse for her transgression.

When using empathic words, make sure you are using a compassionate tone of voice. A sarcastic tone of voice can turn an empathic statement into an angry one. In the next example the dad, Dave, ineffectively gives a consequence to 14-year-old Bobby.

Dave: I let you use my tools yesterday and look what I found lying in the driveway. When will you learn that I mean it when I tell you to put my tools away after you use them? You are grounded from watching any TV the rest of the week. I suppose you think that's harsh? Well, that's really too bad!

Bobby: But it's not fair! I'm going to be totally bored after dinner.

Dave: Gee, that isn't my problem now, is it?

In this situation, Bobby ends up thinking about what a mean dad he has and doesn't even remember what he did that resulted in being punished.

Dave has now learned how to effectively give a consequence:

Dave: Bobby, I just found my tools lying in the driveway. Look, Son, I know it's hard to remember rules sometimes. The rule about putting tools away is really important to me, because my good tools are quite expensive. I'm sorry, I know it's hard, but I'm going to have to remove the computer privileges for today as a consequence. Please try to remember next time, OK?

Bobby: But I'll be bored tonight! I don't know what to do after dinner.

Dave: Son, I'm sorry, I know consequences can be hard to deal with sometimes.

In this situation, Bobby is left feeling frustrated with himself for leaving the tools out, and he makes a resolution to remember the tools rule the next time.

Brief Lines for "Small Stuff" Behaviors

Remember that minor undesirable behaviors should go into the "small stuff" basket and be ignored or receive only low-key interventions. Following are some very brief lines that we find to be quite effective. All of these lines should be said with a loving facial expression and a calm voice, along with a hug or a hand on the shoulder to connect.

• *"I love you too much to argue."* This line is recommended by Cline and Fay (2006, p. 65). It is a wonderful line for ending an argument before it starts, and it conveys the belief that an argument would not be good for your child. If your child keeps arguing, walk away. Your child has developed the arguing habit because he doesn't know healthier ways to engage you in the relationship. Be sure to engage him in normal social conversation whenever you can, so that he learns this method of connecting. If he initiates a normal social conversation, be sure to participate enthusiastically to reinforce his nonarguing methods of engaging you.

• *"I'm trying to believe you, but I'm having a hard time."* This is a wonderful line because it avoids reinforcing the lying behavior by arguing about whether or not the child has lied. In just this one brief comment, you are letting your child know that you would like to give her the benefit of the doubt, that you do suspect she is lying, and that it would mean a lot if she were honest. Another version of the line is, "I would like to believe that," followed by busily moving on to something else. Either line makes it clear to your child that you are fine, that you are moving on, and that the lying behavior is the child's problem.

- *"You know the rules."* This line can be used for many small behaviors. The line makes it clear to your child that you have noticed the behavior, without reinforcing the behavior by excessive attention or arguing. A loving hand on the shoulder and a loving face helps keep the connection. If you believe the behavior warrants a consequence, you might add, "I'm giving you this one reminder." It keeps you out of lecturing or arguing and keeps the behavior as your child's problem, not yours.

To help you refrain from talking too much when your child misbehaves, remember that interrupting negative habits of behavior and adopting new behaviors is a process that takes place over time, through the combination of Integrative Team Treatment and *Integrative Parenting* practices in the home. Your child's therapists will be addressing the misbehaviors through EMDR and family therapy.

In the following vignette, Ronald found that placing 14-year-old Jason's sneaking behaviors in the "small stuff" box was more effective than his previous big reactions to this behavior.

Ronald was a widower raising three teenage sons. He kept a close eye on the time the boys spent playing video and computer games, so they had time for homework, sports, and other activities. Ronald was frustrated with one son, Jason, because Jason continued to sneak extra video/computer playtime whenever he had the chance. Each time Ronald caught Jason sneaking off to his room with a handheld game or getting on a computer game when he was supposed to be doing homework, Ronald sat Jason down and explained why the rules were important and why he was losing trust in Jason, and then he interrogated Jason as to why he was choosing to defy the rules about the games. Ronald tried many consequences, from grounding to removal of privileges. Ronald grew angrier and angrier. The family therapist suggested to Ronald that he use an *Integrative Parenting* strategy by putting the sneaking behavior into the "small stuff" box and sticking to the statement, "You know the rules." He suggested that Ronald present a loving face and a soft voice to maintain the relationship, while holding out his hand for the game or signaling Jason to get back to his homework. The therapist suggested that Ronald walk away quickly after the very brief intervention. Ronald began using the *Integrative Parenting* strategy, and he left all discussion about the behavior for therapy. Gradually, over time, Ronald and Jason grew closer, and Jason's defiance of the rules became less and less frequent.

Set Up Simple Reward Systems

Children can frequently be motivated to work harder at changing a habitual behavior in response to the enticement of a simple reward system. However, there are three mistakes parents often make:

• *Mistake 1.* The reward system is so complicated that it is confusing to the child and even confusing to the parent. The child feels frustrated. He cannot predict when he will gain the rewards and when he will not gain the rewards, so he gives up and feels worse about himself.

• *Mistake 2.* The system is set up to reward vague "good behavior." This feels very random and again confusing to the child. He believes that he really has no control over whether he gets rewards or does not get rewards, so again, he gives up.

• *Mistake 3.* The reward system is too frustrating for the child because the bar is set too high. Commonly, parents will insist that the child behave in the desired way for several days "in a row." To help you understand the internal response of your child, see if you can remember a time you tried to diet, exercise regularly, or give up smoking or some other habit. How many "days in a row" of "good behavior" were you able to achieve? When you felt like you had failed, how long did it take you to throw in the towel and give up?

So the rules of thumb are:

1. *Keep it simple.* Target just one or maybe two behaviors.
2. *Keep it specific.* Target very specific behaviors, such as "getting dressed for school on time" or "getting homework done by 7:00."
3. *Make it achievable.* Choose a behavior that you know your child is capable of successfully manifesting so that she is rewarded sooner rather than later. Place a sticker on the calendar for each time the behavior is achieved. Allow the child to earn a small reward, such as an outing for ice cream or earning

a small item for achieving, say, five stickers—but not in a row. Remember, it's a process of gradually moving your child towards the desired goals.

Following are two examples of the use of simple reward systems for specific behaviors.

• Justine's 10-year-old son Evan was developmentally delayed and suffered from a history of abuse and neglect prior to coming to her home as a foster child when he was 4. With help from the therapist, Justine set up a simple reward system with Evan. She gave Evan a star sticker each morning that he was tantrum-free before school, and each evening that he was tantrum-free after school. When he had earned seven stars, she allowed him to choose a small prize from a prize box. This approach was continued until Evan was tantrum-free most of the time, and then Justine started a new reward system to motivate Evan to pick up the clutter in his room.

• Gabe and Ann set up a simple reward system for 14-year-old Angela. Each night after completing her homework, she was given a point, and when she had earned 10 points, she was allowed to invite a friend to spend the night. They continued the system until she was in the habit of doing homework on a regular basis, and then they set up a new system to encourage her to help with dishes each night.

Give Choices Whenever Possible

Cline and Faye (1990) recommend giving children choices whenever possible to avoid power struggles that are triggered by an authoritarian parenting approach. We view choices as important to brain integration because they force children to light up the thinking areas of the brain, especially when they are having a strong urge to avoid a difficult task or are feeling frustrated by a situation. When parents give choices, they are modeling flexibility and democracy—attitudes we would like our children to adopt, even though we have some firm and fast household rules and expectations. For example, if the rule is "Children get ready for bed at 8:00," parents can give lots of choices around that rule in terms of what pajamas to wear, whether the child takes a shower or a bath, whether to read or just talk at bedtime, and whether to brush teeth before or after the shower. If the rule is "Chores done before dinner," parents can offer a choice in terms of whether to empty or load the dishwasher or whether to bag up the trash or take it to the curb. Choices allow children to feel respected and to feel like they have a voice. Choices teach cooperation, decision-making, and flexibility—all healthy qualities for life.

However, some children are not developmentally ready for choices. Younger children become confused and anxious in the face of choices. Your child may be older chronologically, but developmentally too young to manage the anxiety that accompanies getting to choose. You can tell your child is not ready for choices if she (1) gets to choose but does not follow through with her decision, (2) becomes overwhelmed and cannot choose, or (3) has a meltdown. If this is the case, your child will feel more secure when you are kind but firm and direct, and the rules are simple and very, very clear.

In the following conversation, Brendon's dad helps Brendon use his "thinking brain" by offering him choices. Brendon had brought home a low grade on an algebra test to be signed by his parents. He was visibly upset about the grade.

> **Dad:** Brendon, I know you don't feel good about this grade. Let's do some problem-solving about how you get some help on this algebra and get your grade up.
>
> **Brendon:** I can get it up, Dad. I don't want to talk about it.
>
> **Dad:** Brendon, I can understand that you don't want to talk about it, and we don't have to talk about it right now. What would be better? Would you like to talk a little right after dinner? Or should we talk a little around bedtime?
>
> **Brendon:** Oh, OK, we can talk about it after dinner.

Brendon's dad was quite skillful in that he empathized right away with his son and respected his need to have some space. By giving him a choice about times to talk, it gave Brendon a sense that he did have some control, and allowed for Brendon to become a more collaborative partner in the discussion later.

Use Collaborative Problem-Solving

Ross Greene (2010) promotes a method of de-escalating children's explosions with what he has termed "collaborative problem-solving." We view the method as another way to encourage logical thinking, flexibility, and brain integration. By showing a willingness to really listen to the child's point of view, the child shifts from the "you are mean" stance to a sense that "you are on my side." Any time we help children learn to trust, we are steering them toward healthier relationships. Just notice when your child is beginning to get worked up. No matter what the response, confirm that you understand your child by repeating back exactly what he said. Then express your concern and make a suggestion for brainstorming.

In the following conversation, Steven's dad skillfully implements collaborative problem-solving with him. Steven had entered the house after school and slammed his backpack onto the kitchen counter.

> **Dad:** *(Calmly)* I notice that you are really upset. What's up?
>
> **Steven:** *(Shouting)* That stupid history test was too hard! I'm not retaking that stupid test!
>
> **Dad:** You're angry because that was a really hard test today and you didn't pass and you don't want to have to take it again. *(Invites Steven to sit down and have a snack with him.)* I love you, Son, and I'm concerned for you—I know it doesn't feel good to be so upset, and I know giving up on things won't make you feel very good, either. Do you want milk with those cookies? Let's just relax a bit and talk about other things. Then who knows? Maybe later we could come up with a plan for how to master that darn history test.

This parent first attunes and empathizes with his son to help Steven feel connected and to calm Steven's brain. As Steven gets back into his window of tolerance, he will be able to think more logically and participate in collaborative problem-solving with his father. This parent is definitely helping his son achieve brain integration.

Figure 5.2 is a visual summary of the *Integrative Parenting* style of parenting, which is built upon a foundation of empathy and emotional attunement, play, laughter, and affection to strengthen attachment security, teaching and positive reinforcement to promote positive behaviors, and use of natural and logical consequences with empathy. Compare this figure with Figure 5.1.

IT'S YOUR TURN . . .

1. Pull out your journal and write down any parenting habits you wish to eliminate. Write down *Integrative Parenting* strategies that you would like to use instead.

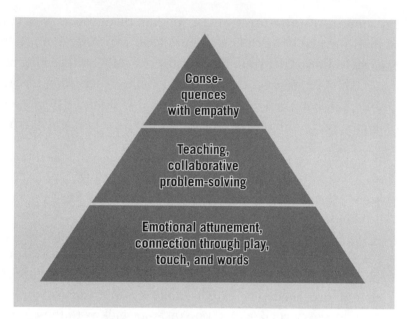

FIGURE 5.2. The *Integrative Parenting* matrix illustrates how a mindful, attuned approach integrates the child's brain by strengthening the relationship, while teaching appropriate skills and behaviors.

2. Make a list of your child's behaviors that belong in the "small stuff" box. Which of the three suggested "brief lines" would be your best response for each of the "small stuff" behaviors?

3. Identify a specific behavior that you would like your child to increase. For example, you want your child to get ready for school in the morning without a tantrum, or you want your child to complete one chore each day. Write out a very simple reward plan to help reinforce that particular behavior.

4. List the behaviors exhibited by your child that you believe warrant a consequence as a motivator for change. Could any of those behaviors be motivated with a reward system instead? If not, write down reasonable consequences that would not last over a day. Do they match the behaviors? Remember that you don't have to give a consequence for every infraction of a rule, and remember that it is most effective to give your child a clean slate each day.

5. Write down two or three empathic statements that you would feel comfortable using when you give a consequence. It is not easy to develop the habit

of using empathic statements, so you will have to stay mindful and intentional with this new practice.

6. Discuss the above plans with your partner to make sure you are parenting as a team. If you don't see eye to eye on everything, enlist the help of the family therapist.

Closing Thoughts

AS SO MANY HAVE SAID, parenting is the most difficult yet most rewarding job a person could have. Parenting a child with attachment trauma provides unique and extraordinarily difficult challenges. These challenges leave many parents overwhelmed, hurt, and questioning their abilities to parent.

Your part is crucial to the success of Integrative Team Treatment for your child, as you help (1) calm his brain, (2) integrate his neurology, and (3) develop his skills for thinking and problem-solving. You can give your child the safety, security, and courage he needs to open up emotionally in therapy, work through his traumatic past, and open his heart to relationships. This is not an overnight fix; it is a process.

Parents like you, who have opened your hearts and homes to this unique population of children, need appreciation, support, and guidance as they navigate the waters of parenting. We hope that this manual proves to be helpful to you on this challenging and meaningful journey.

References

Ainsworth, M. D. S. (1982). Attachment: Retrospect and prospect. In C. M. Parkes & J. Stevenson-Hinde (Eds.), *The place of attachment in human behavior* (pp. 3–29). New York, NY: Tavistock.

American Psychiatric Association. (2013). *Diagnostic and statistical manual of mental disorders* (DSM-5). Washington, DC: Author.

Berk, L. S., Tan, S. A., Fry, W. F., Napier, B. J., Lee, J. W., Hubbard, R. W., et al. (1989). Neuroendocrine and stress hormone changes during mirthful laughter. *American Journal of the Medical Sciences, 298*(6), 390–396.

Bowlby, J. (1973.) *Attachment and loss: Vol. 2. Separation: Anxiety and anger.* New York, NY: Basic Books.

Cline, F., & Fay, J. (1990). *Parenting with love and logic: Teaching children responsibility.* Colorado Springs, CO: Pinon.

Cline, F., & Fay, J. (2006). *Parenting teens with love and logic: Preparing adolescents for responsible adulthood.* Colorado Springs, CO: NavPress.

Cousins, N. (1979). *Anatomy of an illness as perceived by the patient: Reflections on healing and regeneration.* New York, NY: W. W. Norton.

Fonagy, P., Target, M., Steele, M., Steele, H., Leigh, T., Levinson, A., et al. (1997). Morality, disruptive behavior, borderline personality disorder, crime, and their relationships to security of attachment. In L. Atkinson & K. Zucker (Eds.), *Attachment and psychopathology* (pp. 223–274). New York, NY: Guilford Press.

Gottman, J. M., & De Claire, J. (2001). *The relationship cure.* New York, NY: Three Rivers Press.

Greene, R. W. (2010). *The explosive child: A new approach for understanding and parenting easily frustrated, chronically inflexible children.* New York, NY: HarperCollins.

Hughes, D. A. (2006). *Building the bonds of attachment: Awakening love in deeply troubled children.* Northvale, NJ: Aronson.

Kübler-Ross, E., & Kessler, D. (2005). *On grief and grieving: Finding the meaning of grief through the five stages of loss.* New York, NY: Simon & Schuster.

Magid, K., & McKelvey, C. A. (1987). *High risk children without a conscience.* Golden, CO: M & M Publishing.

Main, M., & Solomon, J. (1990). Procedures for identifying infants as disorganized/disoriented during the Ainsworth Strange Situation. In M. Greenberg, D. Cichetti, & M. Cummings (Eds.), *Attachment in the pre-school year* (pp. 121–149). Chicago, IL: University of Chicago Press.

Ogden, P., & Minton, K. (2000). Sensorimotor psychotherapy: One method for processing traumatic memory. *Traumatology, VI* (3), article 3.

Parten, M. (1932). Social participation among preschool children. *Journal of Abnormal and Social Psychology, 28*, 136–147.

Porges, S. W. (2011). *The polyvagal theory: Neurophysiological foundations of emotions, attachment, communication, self-regulation.* New York, NY: Norton.

Post, B. (2012). *Understanding and healing trauma in the adopted child, part 3 of 3.* Retrieved from bryanpost.com/category/adoption–2

Potter, A. E. (2011a). *The anatomy of a meltdown.* Unpublished manuscript.

Potter, A. E. (2011b). *The domino effect.* Unpublished manuscript.

Rizzolatti, G., & Sinigaglia, C. (2008). *Mirrors in the brain: How our minds share actions and emotions.* New York, NY: Oxford University.

Schore, A. N. (1996). *Affect regulation and the origin of the self.* Hillsdale, NJ: Erlbaum.

Shapiro, F. (2007). EMDR and case conceptualization from an adaptive information processing perspective. In F. Shapiro, F. W. Kaslow, & L. Maxfield (Eds.), *Handbook of EMDR and family therapy processes* (pp. 3–34). New York, NY: Guilford Press.

Shapiro, F. (2012). *Getting past your past: Take control of your life with self-help techniques from EMDR therapy.* New York, NY: Rodale.

Siegel, D. J. (1999). *The developing mind: Toward a neurobiology of interpersonal experience.* New York, NY: Guilford Press.

Siegel, D. J. (2001). Toward an interpersonal neurobiology of the developing mind: Attachment relationships, mindsight, and neural integration. *Infant Mental Health Journal, 22*(1–2), 67–94.

Siegel, D. J. (2010). *Mindsight: The new science of personal transformation.* New York, NY: Bantam Books.

Siegel, D. J., & Bryson, T. P. (2011). *The whole-brain child: 12 revolutionary strategies to nurture your child's developing mind.* New York, NY: Bantam Books.

van der Kolk, B. A. (2005). Developmental trauma disorder: Toward a rational diagnosis for children with complex trauma histories. *Psychiatric Annals, 35*(5), 401–408.

Wesselmann, D. (1998). *The whole parent: How to become a terrific parent even if you didn't have one.* Cambridge, MA: Da Capo Press.

Wesselmann, D., Schweitzer, C., & Armstrong, S. (2014). *Integrative team treatment for attachment trauma in children: Family therapy and EMDR.* New York, NY: Norton.

Winnicott, D. (1987). *Babies and their mothers.* Reading, MA: Addison-Wesley.

Index